YORK NOT KT-493-581

...ares (*University*
...shrui (*American*

...return

William Shakespeare

THE WINTER'S TALE

Notes by Loreto Todd

MA (BELFAST) MA PH D (LEEDS)
Lecturer in English, University of Leeds
Senior Lecturer in English, University of Leeds

LONGMAN
YORK PRESS

YORK PRESS
Immeuble Esseily, Place Riad Solh, Beirut

LONGMAN GROUP LIMITED
Longman House, Burnt Mill, Harlow,
Essex CM20 2JE, England
Associated companies, branches and representatives
throughout the world

First published 1980
Thirteenth impression 1994

ISBN 0-582-02323-8

Produced by Longman Singapore Publishers Pte Ltd
Printed in Singapore

Contents

Part 1: Introduction   *page* 5
The Elizabethan age   5
Historical background   5
Social background   6
William Shakespeare, 1564–1616   7
Background notes on Elizabethan drama   8
Contemporary dramatists   9
The Elizabethan theatre   11
Shakespeare's English   13
Shakespeare's plays   19
The nature of tragicomedy   20
Title and history of *The Winter's Tale*   21
A note on the text   23

Part 2: Summaries   24
A general summary   24
Detailed summaries   25
Concluding comments   61

Part 3: Commentary   63
Character evaluation   63
Poetic language   84
The effect of *The Winter's Tale*   88

Part 4: Hints for study   89
Studying *The Winter's Tale*   89
Answering questions   89
Specimen questions and suggested answers   91
Revision questions   96

Part 5: Suggestions for further reading   98
The author of these notes   99

Part 1

Introduction

The Elizabethan age

Queen Elizabeth I came to the throne in 1558 and ruled England until 1603. Her reign brought stability to the country and with stability came prosperity. In order to see how necessary peace and order were to the Elizabethans, it is useful to contrast Elizabeth's reign with the insecurity and unrest of earlier ages.

Historical background

Elizabeth's grandfather, Henry Tudor, became King Henry VII of England in 1485. His accession and subsequent marriage to Elizabeth of York put an end to the civil wars which had racked England for almost a hundred years. Henry VII concentrated on reducing friction at home and abroad and on establishing a strong, financially secure monarchy.

He was succeeded in 1509 by his son Henry VIII who married a Spanish princess, Catherine of Aragon. This marriage did not produce a son and so Henry VIII divorced her. The divorce was condemned by the Catholic Church and, gradually, a split developed between the Pope and Henry. Henry died in 1547 and at that time England was still largely a Catholic country, Catholic that is in practice, though the supreme spiritual authority of the Pope had been challenged, and many Protestant reformers were eager to spread Protestantism in England.

Henry VIII was succeeded by his nine-year-old son Edward and his Regents furthered the spread of Protestantism. Edward died in 1553 and was followed to the throne by his half-sister Mary, daughter of Catherine of Aragon and a devout Catholic. She attempted to restore Catholicism to England but she died childless and was succeeded in 1558 by her Protestant half-sister Elizabeth.

Elizabeth adopted what might be called a 'middle way' as far as religion was concerned. She broke the link with Rome but retained many of the practices and beliefs of the old religion. Her 'middle way' satisfied most of her subjects and for the majority of her reign religious strife was avoided. Many different Christian sects became established in England during her reign, however, among them the Puritans who were very critical of the theatre.

Social background

In spite of the political and religious turmoil of the reigns prior to Elizabeth's most Elizabethans were convinced that they lived in an ordered universe, a universe in which God was supreme and in which angels, men, animals, plants and stones had their allotted place. The Christian view that mankind was redeemed by Christ was rarely challenged by Elizabethans, though points of detail might be argued about. In spite of the teaching that Adam's fall had, to some extent, spoiled God's plan for mankind, there was a widely held belief in universal order and harmony. The stars and the planets were still in accord with the divine plan and it was believed that they gave glory to God by the music of their movement. Shakespeare expresses this idea in his play *The Merchant of Venice* when Lorenzo tells Jessica:

> Look how the floor of heaven
> Is thick inlaid with patines of bright gold;
> There's not the smallest orb which thou behold'st
> But in his motion like an angel sings,
> Still quiring to the young-ey'd cherubins;
> Such harmony is in immortal souls,
> But whilst this muddy vesture of decay
> Doth grossly close it in, we cannot hear it.
> (V.1.58–65)

Before Adam's fall, man too could hear the heavenly harmonies. Although the fall put an end to this ideal state, the heavenly bodies continued to influence life on earth. Just as the sun gave warmth and light, just as the moon caused the tidal movement of the seas, so too did the stars and planets affect the earth and its inhabitants. Most Elizabethans attributed certain types of behaviour to astrological causes such as the sign of the zodiac under which a person was born or the relative positions of the planets at a particular time. There is evidence of such a belief in *The Winter's Tale*. Mercury was thought to be associated with trickery, subtlety, vitality and commerce. Autolycus was a mercurial man and he attributed his character to the influence of Mercury. As he put it:

> My father named me Autolycus, who, being as I am, littered under Mercury, was likewise a snapper-up of unconsidered trifles. (IV.3. 24–6)

Shakespeare's contemporaries, like many people before and since then, were aware of man's paradoxical position in nature. A man was influenced by the stars and planets, subject to his passions and, at the same time, made in the image and likeness of God. This duality in human nature is aptly summed up in *The Essay on Man* (1733) a poem by Alexander Pope (1688-1744). Pope describes man as:

> *Great lord of all things, yet a prey to all;*
> *Sole judge of Truth, in endless Error hurled;*
> *The glory, jest, and riddle of the world.*
>   (Epistle II, 16-18)

Man was most in harmony with nature and with his creator, it was believed, when his reason controlled his emotions. A similar truth was believed to apply to the state. Natural disorders, like storms and earthquakes, were paralleled by passionate outbursts in the individual and by disputes in the state. These views are most clearly seen in such plays of Shakespeare as *King Lear* and *Othello* where storms and bad weather symbolise the turmoil and confusion of the characters, but they were commonly held in Elizabethan times. We see some evidence of these views in *The Winter's Tale* in that Leontes's jealousy causes dissension in his kingdom and results in the death of his male heir.

The reigns of Elizabeth and James I were marked by increased public discussion of religion and of the extent of God's intervention in human affairs. *The Winter's Tale*, like the other plays written at the end of Shakespeare's career, plays such as *Pericles*, *Cymbeline* and *The Tempest*, is concerned with such themes as the conquest of evil by good, the value of repentance and reconciliation, the beauty of innocence and the direct involvement of supernatural forces in the affairs of man.

William Shakespeare, 1564-1616

We know very little about who Shakespeare was or how he lived. And, apart from the ideas expressed in his writings, we know nothing at all about what he thought or how he reacted to the events of his time. He was born in Stratford-upon-Avon in Warwickshire and was baptised there on 26 April 1564. His father, John Shakespeare, seems to have been reasonably wealthy at the time of William's birth. He had business interests in farming, butchering, wool-dealing and glove-making and he held several public offices in Stratford until about 1578 when his business began to decline.

It seems likely, in view of his father's position, that William was educated at the Stratford Grammar School. He did not, however, go to university and so did not have the type of education which many contemporary playwrights had.

William Shakespeare married Anne Hathaway in 1582 when he was eighteen and she twenty-six and, by 1585, they had three children, Susanna, born shortly after the marriage, and twins Judith and Hamnet born in 1585. We cannot be certain how Shakespeare supported his family during this time. He may have been involved in his father's diminishing business or he may, as some traditions suggest, have been a schoolmaster. Whatever he did, however, it did not satisfy him completely because he left Stratford and went to London.

Once again, we cannot be sure when Shakespeare moved to London. It may have been in 1585, the year when a group of London players visited Stratford and performed their plays there. But we do know that he was living in London in 1592, by which time he was already known as a dramatist and an actor. Indeed, even at this early date, his plays must have been popular because, in 1592, Shakespeare was criticised in a pamphlet by a less successful writer, Robert Greene, who wrote that a new and largely uneducated dramatist (that is, Shakespeare) was usurping the position which rightly belonged to university men.

Plague broke out in London in 1593 and all theatres were closed. Shakespeare seems to have used the time of the closure to write two long poems, 'The Rape of Lucrece' and 'Venus and Adonis' and to strengthen his relationship with a theatre group called the Lord Chamberlain's Company in Elizabeth's reign and the King's Men after the accession of James I in 1603. Shakespeare maintained his association with this company until he retired from the theatre and he seems to have prospered with it.

In 1596 came personal grief and achievement. His son Hamnet died, and Shakespeare and his father were granted a coat of arms which meant that their status as 'gentlemen' was recognised by the College of Heralds. In the following year, 1597, Shakespeare bought New Place, one of the largest houses in Stratford. In 1599 he bought shares in the Globe Theatre and, in 1609, he became part owner of the newly built Blackfriars Theatre. In this year also he published a collection of sonnets. Shakespeare retired to New Place in 1611 though he did not break all his business contacts with London. He died in Stratford on 23 April 1616 at the age of fifty-two.

Background notes on Elizabethan drama

Records of drama in English go back to the Middle Ages, a period in which numerous 'miracle' and 'morality' plays were written. Such plays were often based on biblical themes, especially those involving miraculous events such as the saving of Noah and his family in the ark, or those from which a clear moral could be drawn. Medieval plays were usually written to coincide with such religious festivals as Christmas or Easter and they were often performed in or near the church, with most of the community taking part either actively, by playing a role, or passively, as a member of the audience.

In the medieval period drama was an integral element in the structure of society. It was, in many ways, an extension of Christian ritual and was meant to make a strong impression on all who participated in the performances. Audiences were intended to be awed by the power and wisdom of God, inspired by the faith and courage of holy men, frightened by the fate of evil-doers and amused by the folly of mankind. Drama in the period was thus meant to have a cathartic effect, that is, it was intended to improve the members of the audience by giving them an outlet for such emotions as greed, hatred, lust and pity. The audience was encouraged to sympathise with a frequently used character called Everyman who represented all men in their journey through life. The drama of the time, like Everyman himself, had a universal appeal. It was written, not for a small élite, but with all members of the society in mind.

In the early sixteenth century the close relationship that had previously existed between Church and State began to change. Individual Christian sects had distinctly different attitudes to the role of drama in society. It was tolerated by Catholics but condemned by Puritans who wished to 'purify' religious beliefs and attitudes and to encourage people to give up worldly pleasures so that they might attend to spiritual matters. Puritanism grew stronger, especially in towns and cities, in the second half of the sixteenth century and people connected with drama—writers and actors—had to struggle against growing opposition. Elizabethan dramatists often criticised puritanism in their plays and there is some evidence of such criticism in several of Shakespeare's plays, including *Twelfth Night*. Puritanical opposition to the theatre eventually succeeded in curtailing freedom of speech in drama when they sponsored the Licensing Act which was passed by Parliament in 1737.

In Shakespeare's day, however, the theatre had the support of the Court and many dramatists, including Shakespeare, continued the medieval tradition of producing plays which appealed to all classes and to different levels of intelligence and education.

Contemporary dramatists

Numerous Englishmen wrote plays in the sixteenth century, men such as John Lyly (*c*.1554–1606), Thomas Kyd (1558–94), Robert Greene (1558–92) and Thomas Nashe (1567–1601). Among the most talented of these dramatists was Christopher Marlowe (1564–93). He was born in the same year as Shakespeare but seems to have begun writing plays before Shakespeare did. He was a gifted poet and many of his dramatic innovations were adopted by playwrights of his own and later generations. He was the first English dramatist to make effective and extensive use of blank verse, that is, he frequently used an organised pattern of rhythm in his plays giving his verse the memorability of poetry and the effortlessness of natural speech:

> The stars move still, time runs, the clock will strike,
> The devil will come, and Faustus must be damned.
> O I'll leap up to my God: who pulls me down?
> See, see where Christ's blood streams in the firmament.
> One drop would save my soul, half a drop, ah my Christ.
> (*Doctor Faustus*, 1588–9, lines 1429–1433)

Marlowe was the forerunner of Shakespeare in that he centred his

THE GLOBE PLAYHOUSE

The theatre, originally built by James Burbage in 1576, was made of wood (Burbage had been trained as a carpenter). It was situated to the north of the River Thames on Shoreditch in Finsbury Fields. There was trouble with the lease of the land, and so the theatre was dismantled in 1598, and reconstructed 'in another forme' on the south side of the Thames as the Globe. Its sign is thought to have been a figure of the Greek hero Hercules carrying the globe. It was built in six months, its galleries being roofed with thatch. This caught fire in 1613 when some smouldering wadding, from a cannon used in a performance of Shakespeare's *Henry VIII*, lodged in it. The theatre was burnt down, and when it was rebuilt again on the old foundations, the galleries were roofed with tiles.

tragedies on one main character, a character with whom the audience could identify, but he was closer than Shakespeare to the medieval tradition in that his characters tend to behave like supernatural beings.

Shakespeare seems to have learned much from his contemporaries, especially Marlowe, and from the medieval dramatic tradition. He borrowed plots and ideas from many sources but they were transformed by his poetry and his dramatic talents.

The Elizabethan theatre

Drama became increasingly secularised during the fifteenth and sixteenth centuries and plays ceased to be performed in or near a church. Instead, they were often staged in the courtyard of an inn.

Putting on a performance in such a courtyard had several advantages. There were many doors which could be used for exits and entrances, balconies which could represent battlements or towers and, best of all, perhaps, there were usually guests in the inns who were glad of entertainment.

When the first theatre was built in London, in 1576, it seemed perfectly natural, therefore, to build it according to the design of Elizabethan courtyards. The theatre had galleries and boxes around the walls where the wealthy sat, and like the courtyard of an inn, it had no roof and so performances were cancelled when the weather was bad. The 1576 theatre and those built subsequently differed from the courtyard in that they contained a large stage—often called an 'apron' stage because of its shape—which jutted out from one wall into the auditorium. The poorer members of the audience were called 'groundlings' and they stood around the stage throughout the performance.

The large apron stage was not curtained from the audience and there was no scenery on it. Indications of where the scene occurred were built into the words of the play. In Act III, Scene 1 of *The Winter's Tale*, for example, Cleomenes, in discussing the Oracle at Delphi (or Delphos) with Dion, indirectly tells the audience where they are and what the weather is like:

> The climate's delicate, the air most sweet,
> Fertile the isle, the temple much surpassing
> The common praise it bears.
> (III.2.1–3)

Similar information is provided for the audience by Antigonus and the mariner when the scene changes to Bohemia:

> ANTIGONUS: Thou art perfect, then, our ship hath touch'd upon
> The deserts of Bohemia?

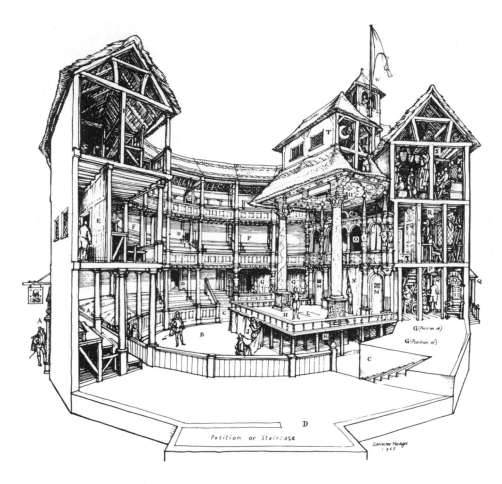

A CONJECTURAL RECONSTRUCTION OF THE INTERIOR OF THE GLOBE PLAYHOUSE

AA Main entrance
B The Yard
CC Entrances to lowest gallery
D Entrance to staircase and upper galleries
E Corridor serving the different sections of the middle gallery
F Middle gallery ('Twopenny Rooms')
G 'Gentlemen's Rooms' or Lords' Rooms'
H The stage
J The hanging being put up round the stage
K The 'Hell' under the stage
L The stage trap, leading down to the Hell
MM Stage doors

N Curtained 'place behind the stage'
O Gallery above the stage, used as required sometimes by musicians, sometimes by spectators, and often as part of the play
P Back-stage area (the tiring-house)
Q Tiring-house door
R Dressing-rooms
S Wardrobe and storage
T The hut housing the machine for lowering enthroned gods, etc., to the stage
U The 'Heavens'
W Hoisting the playhouse flag

MARINER: Ay, my lord, and fear
We have landed in ill time: the skies look grimly,
And threaten present blusters.
                    (III.3.1-4)

The lack of scenery was also, in part, compensated for by the use of very rich costumes and music.

In the sixteenth and early seventeenth centuries, it seems likely that plays went on from beginning to end without interval though the end of a scene is often indicated by the use of such expressions as:

. . . Come sir, away. (I.2.465)

. . . Leave me. (II.3.205)

and:

. . . Come, and lead me
To these sorrows. (III.2.242-3)

In Shakespeare's time, women were not allowed to perform on the public stage, and therefore female roles were played by boys. This fact helps to explain why so many of Shakespeare's heroines, heroines such as Portia in *The Merchant of Venice*, Rosalind in *As You Like It* and Viola in *Twelfth Night*, disguise themselves as young men. It was easier for a boy to act like a young man than to act like a young woman.

Shakespeare's English

Every living language changes. Differences in pronunciation and in linguistic performance are often apparent even in the speech of a father and his son, so it is not surprising that the language of Shakespeare's plays should be markedly different from the English we use today. In the sixteenth century, the English language was only beginning to be used by creative writers. Previously, Latin and French had been considered more suitable for literary expression and consequently the English language had not been as fully developed as it might have been. Because of this the language of Shakespeare and his contemporaries was used less systematically than it is today.

The main differences between Shakespearean and modern English can be considered under the following headings:

(1) Mobility of word classes

Adjectives, nouns and verbs were less rigidly confined to their specific classes in Shakespeare's day. Adjectives were often used as adverbs. In Act III, Scene 2, 186-7 Paulina criticises Leontes, proclaiming:

> That did but show thee, of a fool, inconstant
> And *damnable* ingrateful:

where modern usage would require 'damnably ungrateful'. Adjectives could also be used as nouns. In Act II, Scene 1, 94, Leontes speaks of: '... *vulgars* ...' where today he would say 'vulgar people' or 'common people'.

Nouns were often used as verbs. In Act I, Scene 2, 313–14 Leontes insists:

> I from meaner form
> Have *benched* and reared to worship,

where the noun 'bench' is used as if it were a verb with the meaning of 'give a seat to/raise to a higher position'; and verbs were also, on occasions, used as nouns. In Act II, Scene 3, 169–71, for example, 'fail' is used in a context where today we would need 'failure':

> ... for the *fail*
> Of any point in't shall not only be
> Death to thyself, but to thy lewd-tongued wife.

---

(2) Changes in the meaning of words

Words change their meanings as time passes, and thus many words used by Shakespeare have different values today. Such changes can be illustrated by the following examples. 'Affection' which now means 'love, liking, fondness' could mean 'quality, characteristics' in Shakespeare's day and this is the sense in which it is used in Act V, Scene 2, 36–8:

> ... the majesty of the creature
> in resemblance of the mother, the *affection* of nobleness
> which nature shows above her breeding, ...

'Countenance' now usually only refers to the face but in Shakespeare's writings it could mean 'appearance', a meaning it has in Act V, Scene 2, 48–9:

> ... with *countenance* of such
> distraction, ...

And 'Ethiopian' was used to mean 'negro' or 'African' rather than someone from Ethiopia:

> ... I take thy hand, this hand,
> As soft as dove's down and as white as it,
> Or *Ethiopian*'s tooth,
> (IV.4.363–5)

(3) Vocabulary loss

Not only do words change in meaning in a living language, some also cease to be used. Many words which occur in Shakespeare are no longer current in modern English. This is true of the following items in *The Winter's Tale*:

barne (III,3,69)	child
bawcock (I.2.121)	fine fellow
blench (I.2.333)	move from the correct path
boiled-brains (III.3.64)	hotheads, fools
boot (IV.4.638)	compensation
to boot (I.2.80)	as well, in addition
bourn (I.2.134)	limit, boundary
caddisses (IV.4.209)	tapes often used to make garters
callat (II.3.90)	loose woman
cap-a-pe (IV.4.736)	from head to foot
carbonadoed (IV.4.266)	cut and marked as for cooking
clipping (V.2.55)	embracing, kissing
collop (I.2.137)	piece of meat, flesh and blood
discase (IV.4.634)	undress, remove one's clothes
disliken (IV.4.652)	disguise
doxy (IV.3.2)	female beggar, beggar's girl-friend
fantastical (IV.4.752)	strange, odd
fardel (IV.4.707)	burden, bundle
i'fecks (I.2.120)	in faith; 'i'fecks' was a mild oath
fedary (II.1.90)	a person in league with another, accomplice
gallimaufry (IV.4.329)	confused jumble
gest (I.2.41)	a scheduled stop on a journey or pilgrimage, the time taken for such a stop
gillyvors (IV.4.82)	a flower, a type of carnation
gust (I.2.219)	realise, appreciate
hand-fast (IV.4.769)	under arrest
hefts (II.1.45)	shakes, heavings
incertain (V.1.29)	insecure, unsure
inkles (IV.4.209)	linen tapes
lozel (II.3.108)	rascal, scoundrel
lunes (II.2.30)	attacks of lunacy
moe (I.2.8)	more
nayward (II.1.64)	contrary, tendency to say 'no'
neat (I.2.123)	cow, cattle
neb (I.2.183)	impolite word for 'mouth'
oxlips (IV.4.125)	large cowslips
paddling (I.2.115)	the holding of hands by lovers

partlet (II.3.75)	hen
pash (I.2.128)	head
pettitoes (IV.4.608)	pig's trotters
placket (IV.4.611)	large pocket; the term was sometimes applied to a woman's private parts, petticoat
pugging (IV.3.7)	stealing
purblind (I.2.228)	totally blind
quoifs (IV.4.226)	close-fitting caps
scape (III.3.71)	sin
sneaping (I.2.13)	nipping
tired (II.3.74)	pulled apart, torn
three-pile (IV.3.14)	very thick, expensive velvet
tods (IV.3.32)	quantities of wool; a 'tod' was usually equivalent to 28 pounds weight
troth-plight (I.2.278)	engagement, betrothal
welkin (I.2.136)	sky, heavens
wotting (III.2.76)	knowing

The difficulties posed by changes of meaning and loss of vocabulary can easily be exaggerated. The majority of words that occur in Shakespeare's plays are still used today and their meanings are usually made clear by their context.

---

(4) Verbs

Shakespearean verb forms differ from modern usage in three main ways. Firstly, questions and negatives could be formed without using 'do' or 'did'. Thus, in Act I, Scene 2, 146 Polixenes asks Leontes: 'What *means* Sicilia?' where today one would have to say: 'What *does* the King of Sicilia *mean*?' Similarly, in Act II, Scene 1, 163–4 Leontes claims:

> Our prerogative
> *Calls* not your counsels,

thus using a construction which is not acceptable in modern English. One must add, however, that Shakespeare often formed questions and negatives as we do today. In Act I, Scene 2, 377 Polixenes asks: '*Do* you know . . .?' and in Act II, Scene 2, 39–40 Emilia suggests:

> We *do not know*
> How he may soften at the sight o'th' child:

Whereas, however, Shakespeare could use both:

1(*a*) Like you it?   and   1(*b*) Do you like it?
2(*a*) I like it not   and   2(*b*) I do not like it

3(*a*) Liked you it?　and　　3(*b*) Did you like it?
4(*a*) I liked it not　　and　　4(*b*) I did not like it

modern English only permits the (*b*) forms.

Secondly, some past tense forms are used which would be ungrammatical today. In *The Winter's Tale* such examples as the following occur:

'beat' for 'beaten':
He's *beat* from his best ward. (I.2.33)

'forgot' for 'forgotten':
O Perdita, what have we twain *forgot*? (IV.4.660)

and 'spoke' for 'spoken':
Why lo you now; I have *spoke* to th' purpose twice: (I.2.106).

Thirdly, archaic forms of verbs sometimes occur with 'thou' and with third person singular subjects including 'that/he/she/it':

Dost thou hear, Camillo? (I.2.399)

What! *canst* not rule her? (II.3.46)

　　　A gross hag!
And, lozel, thou *art* worthy to be hang'd,
That *wilt* not stay her tongue.
　　　　　(II.3.107-9)

and:

　　　So please you, sir, their speed
Hath been beyond account.
　　　　　(II.3.196-7)

(5) Pronouns

Shakespeare's pronoun usage differs to some extent from our own. There was a certain amount of choice in the use of second person pronouns in Shakespeare's day. 'You' had to be used when more than one person was addressed and so the officer uses 'you' when he puts Cleomenes and Dion on oath:

You here shall swear upon this sword of justice,
That *you*, Cleomenes and Dion, have
Been both at Delphos,
　　　　　(III.2.124-6)

The use of 'you' could also indicate respect. Thus Florizel and Perdita show their mutual respect by addressing each other as 'you':

FLORIZEL: These *your* unusual weeds, to each part of *you*
Do give a life: no shepherdess, but Flora
Peering in April's front. This *your* sheep-shearing
Is as a meeting of the petty gods,
And *you* the queen on't.
PERDITA: Sir: my gracious lord,
To chide at *your* extremes, it not becomes me—
(IV.4.1-6)

though, later in the scene, Florizel indicates his strong attachment to Perdita by changing from 'you' to 'thou':

Thou dearest Perdita,
With these forced thoughts, I prithee, darken not
The mirth o' th' feast. (IV.4.40-2)

Superiors often used 'thou' to their inferiors and were, in return, addressed as 'you'. Antigonus, for example, asks the mariner:

Thou art perfect, then, our ship hath touched upon
The deserts of Bohemia? (III.3.1-2)

whereas, the mariner uses the respectful pronoun to Antigonus:

Make *your* best haste, and go not
Too far i' th' land: (III.3.10-11)

Thus, the use of 'thou' could, depending on the situation, suggest intimacy or condescension. When used inappropriately, however, 'thou' could imply an insult. So, when Sir Toby Belch, in Shakespeare's *Twelfth Night*, encourages Sir Andrew Aguecheek to challenge Cesario to a duel, he says:

. . . taunt him with the license of ink: if *thou thou'st* him some thrice, it shall not be amiss . . . (that is, if you use the 'thou' form he will be insulted and may accept your challenge). (III.2.42-3)

A further pronominal difference which may be noted is the use of 'it' to refer to a person. In Act I, Scene 1, 35 Archidamus describes Mamillius as:

. . . *it* is a gentleman of
the greatest promise that ever came into my note.

And in Act II, Scene 3, 77-9 Paulina uses 'it' in referring to Perdita:

Unvenerable be thy hands, if thou
Tak'st up the princess, by that forced baseness
Which he has put upon'*t*!

(6) Prepositions

In Shakespeare's lifetime prepositional usage was less standardised than it is now and so many of his prepositions differ from those we would employ today. Among these are:

'of' for 'for':
> That did but show thee, *of* a fool, inconstant (III.2.186)

'in' for 'at':
> *In* many singularities; (that is, at its many wonders) (V.3.12)

'on' for 'in':
> I smell the trick *on*'t. (IV.4.643)

'on' for 'at':
> I know by the picking
> *on*'s teeth. (IV.4.753–4).

(7) Multiple negation

In modern English we use only one negative in a sentence but in Shakespeare's day two or even more negatives could be used for emphasis. In his sonnet *Let me not to the marriage of true minds*, for example, Shakespeare concludes with the following couplet:

> If this be error and upon me proved,
> I *never* writ, *nor no* man ever loved.

In *The Winter's Tale* we find many examples of double negatives, among them the following:

> *Nor* night, *nor* day, *no* rest: it is but weakness
>   (II.3.1)

and:

> I say she's dead: I'll swear 't. If word *nor* oath
> Prevail *not*, go and see:
>   (III.2.203–4)

Shakespeare's plays

Shakespeare's creative period as a dramatist spans approximately twenty years, from 1591 to 1611. During this time he is believed to have written thirty-seven plays and he may have collaborated with other playwrights in the writing of a number of others. It is not always easy to know when individual plays were written but some idea of dating can be gained from records of performances, from the order given in editions published before and shortly after Shakespeare's death. It is on the basis of such evidence that scholars suggest 1611 as the probable date for the composition of *The Winter's Tale*.

Shakespeare's plays were not 'original' in the modern sense of 'new'. Many of his plots were borrowed from history or from contemporary literature but they were moulded by him into unique and successful plays. These can be divided into two main types, comedies which had happy endings and tragedies which involved the death of the chief character. In his final works, however, Shakespeare often combined sad and joyful events in plays which have come to be classified as 'tragicomedies'.

The nature of tragicomedy

Shakespearean comedies usually dealt with the happier aspects of life such as love and marriage, often, as in *The Winter's Tale*, making lavish use of music and singing. Frequently, there were two levels in the comedy, one involving the love interests of courtly characters, in this case Florizel and Perdita, and another treating the humorous behaviour of less elevated personalities such as Autolycus and the Clown.

Tragedies, however, were concerned with the harsher side of life, with the trials and eventual death of an important person. Often the hero's fall from happiness was due to a weakness in his character, a weakness such as the overweening ambition of Macbeth or the uncontrolled jealousy of Othello.

In *The Winter's Tale* we have a combination of the two types of play. Love is a central theme as it is in such comedies by Shakespeare as *Much Ado About Nothing* and *As You Like It*; music is an essential part of the play and the words of some of the songs are an integral part of the dialogue (see, for example, IV.3.13–26) and yet the audience is made aware of the less joyful possibilities of life. Evil is clearly shown to exist. The unprovoked jealousy of Leontes causes the trial and degradation of Hermione, the deaths of Mamillius and Antigonus, and the banishment of Perdita. His impetuous behaviour could have deprived him of all hope of happiness but the seeds of doom are not allowed to develop and the play ends with the reconciliation of the major characters and with the suggestion that the love between Perdita and Florizel has helped to compensate for the strife between their fathers.

Prose is sometimes used for comic episodes as in Act IV, Scene 3, 23–118, for example, whereas blank verse is the usual medium for more serious interaction. By alternating between prose and poetry Shakespeare can emphasise differences in language and behaviour while, at the same time, implying the essential similarity between the needs and urges of all his characters and stressing the common humanity they share with their audience.

Title and history of *The Winter's Tale*

It seems possible that Shakespeare selected the title of *The Winter's Tale* because it was simple, easy to remember and likely to arouse the curiosity of his audience. To most of Shakespeare's contemporaries a 'winter's tale' would suggest a strange, perhaps magical, story that was old, long and very suitable for passing the time on a winter's evening. Because winter was the season of darkness and death winter's tales are often sad but, just as winter heralded spring, there was sometimes a suggestion in such tales that joy and growth replaced barren misery.

In Shakespeare's play, there are three specific references to winter tales. In Act II, Scene 1 Mamillius agrees to tell his mother and her ladies a story and adds:

A sad tale's best for winter: I have one
Of sprites and goblins (25–6)

a comment which, in the light of subsequent events, suggests dramatic irony. The other two references come towards the end of the play and stress the incredible nature of the events which culminate in Hermione's 'resurrection', Perdita's reinstatment as Princess and the reconciliation between the royal houses of Sicilia and Bohemia. A courtier insists:

This news,
which is called true, is so like an old tale that the
verity of it is in strong suspicion
(V.2.27–9)

and Paulina emphasises the same point in the next scene when she says of Hermione:

That she is living,
Were it but told you, should be hooted at
Like an old tale.
(V.3.115–7)

Shakespeare's use of 'the' in the title of his play suggests that he is not dealing with just *any* tale but rather with the quintessential winter's tale. Perhaps the audience was meant to see the parallel between spring's conquest of winter and the victory of love and reconciliation over hatred and discord.

The Winter's Tale was one of Shakespeare's last plays and it seems likely that it was written early in 1611. It was performed at the Globe

Theatre on 15 May 1611, and so we know that it was written before that date. Although we cannot be certain how much before 15 May 1611 it was written, the tragicomic nature of the play, its development of the themes of repentance and reconciliation, its use of songs which are carefully integrated into the plot and dialogue, all suggest that the play was written towards the end of Shakespeare's career. The play was performed at court in 1613 as part of the wedding celebrations for Princess Elizabeth and it has always been reasonably popular, although some critics have suggested that, as a play, *The Winter's Tale* is poorly constructed (see pp. 61–2).

In writing his plays, Shakespeare frequently made use of contemporary literature and this is certainly true of *The Winter's Tale* which derives its plot from a prose romance called *Pandosto*. *Pandosto* was written by Robert Greene and published in 1588. It proved very popular and so was reprinted several times during the sixteenth and seventeenth centuries. Shakespeare followed the outline of Greene's plot quite closely. In both *Pandosto* and *The Winter's Tale* a king's unfounded jealousy causes death and disorder. In both, the love between members of the younger generation helps to compensate for the animosity between their parents. But, although Shakespeare owed much of his plot to Greene, he adapted it to suit his own purposes. He changed the names of the characters and much of the action. In *Pandosto*, for example, the wronged queen dies and the king commits suicide. In *The Winter's Tale* Hermione only seems to die and she, her daughter and the king are eventually reunited and the marriage between Perdita and Florizel suggests that harmony will also prevail between the kingdoms.

Apart from *Pandosto* it seems that Shakespeare also made use of contemporary pamphlets on rogues and their behaviour, especially Greene's pamphlets (1592) which describe how pickpockets often sang to attract a large crowd. Much of this information is incorporated into the scenes involving Autolycus, a character who has no counterpart in Greene's romance.

It would be fair to say that Shakespeare drew much of his inspiration for *The Winter's Tale* from *Pandosto* and from tracts relating to rogues, but, as with all his writings, Shakespeare absorbed such influences creating a play which transformed his sources.

A note on the text

The Winter's Tale first appeared in the First Folio of 1623 where it is placed with the Comedies, suggesting perhaps that the publishers classified it according to its happy ending. The Folio text is clear and accurate. It divides the play into Acts and Scenes and also provides stage directions. All subsequent editions have been based on the text of the First Folio although the majority of recent printings have modernised the spelling. The main difference between modern editions occurs in the numbering of the lines. The Acts and the Scenes are the same but the number of prose lines differs depending on the size of the print and the width of the page. The Arden Edition* of *The Winter's Tale* has been used for all quotations. Its text has been modified only in so far as the apostrophe has been replaced by 'e' in such verbal forms as:

> proclaim'd (I.2.32)
> call'd   (I.2.125).

If the student uses a different text it should not be hard to find the quoted lines in his own edition.

---

* *The Winter's Tale*, The Arden Edition of the Works of William Shakespeare, edited by J.H.P. Pafford, Methuen, London, 1976

Part 2

Summaries
of THE WINTER'S TALE

A general summary

At the beginning of the play we learn that King Leontes of Sicilia has been entertaining his friend, King Polixenes of Bohemia. While Polixenes is still his guest, Leontes is overcome by feelings of jealousy. He believes that his wife, Hermione, has been unfaithful to him and suspects that Polixenes has been her lover. Accordingly, Leontes orders one of his courtiers, Camillo, to poison Polixenes. Camillo, who believes that Hermione and Polixenes are innocent, warns the King of Bohemia of his danger and he and Polixenes secretly leave the court of Leontes.·

When Leontes discovers that they have escaped he becomes even more convinced of his wife's guilt. He puts Hermione in prison to await trial and sends messengers to consult the Oracle of Apollo at Delphos. Leontes does not wait for the Oracle's verdict, however. He believes that Hermione has committed adultery and so he disowns the daughter that Hermione gives birth to in prison. He orders Antigonus, another Sicilian courtier, to burn the child but is eventually persuaded that the child should simply be abandoned. Antigonus leaves the baby in a remote spot on the shores of Bohemia where she is found by a shepherd and brought up as his own daughter.

In the meantime, Hermione's trial begins. During the trial the messengers return with the Oracle's judgement which declares that Hermione is innocent. Leontes refuses to accept this testimony saying:

There is no truth at all i' th' Oracle:
The sessions shall proceed: this is mere falsehood.
    (III.2.140–41)

He has barely uttered the blasphemy when he is told that his son, Mamillius, has died. Hermione faints when she hears the news of her son's death and later Leontes is informed that she too is dead. The King suddenly realises that he has been unjust and he begins to mourn for the loss of his family, his friend and his happiness.

Sixteen years pass before we meet any of the characters again. The abandoned child has grown into a very beautiful young woman, called Perdita, and Florizel, the son of King Polixenes, has met and fallen in love with her. Polixenes does not approve of his son's love for a shepherdess and orders Florizel to put an end to the romance. Florizel, however, prefers to give up his claim to the throne rather than lose Perdita. They follow Camillo's advice and flee to the court of King Leontes in the hope that he will help them.

The old shepherd who has cared for Perdita for sixteen years is taken by force to Sicilia. He manages to convince the court that Perdita is the daughter of Leontes. This happy discovery is augmented by the good news that Hermione is still alive. The play ends with Hermione restored to Leontes and with the promise that the two royal families will be united by a marriage between Florizel and Perdita.

Detailed summaries

Act I Scene 1

This short introductory scene is used to inform the audience that Polixenes, the King of Bohemia, is on a visit to the court of Leontes, the King of Sicilia. The two courtiers, Camillo and Archidamus, stress the facts that Leontes and Polixenes have been friends since childhood and that the visit has been an extremely happy one.

NOTES AND GLOSSARY:

Bohemia: in Shakespeare's day Bohemia was a country in central Europe covering much of the area now known as Czechoslovakia. It would be foolish, however, to equate Polixenes's kingdom with any geographical entity. The choice of both Sicilia and Bohemia was suggested by *Pandosto* and Shakespeare simply intended them to represent European kingdoms

on the like occasion: in similar circumstances

Bohemia: Polixenes. Shakespeare frequently uses the name of a country for its king. In line 21 'Sicilia' designates Leontes

visitation: visit

Wherein our ... loves: although our ability to entertain you will not be of a high standard, we shall make up for this lack by our affection

unintelligent of our insufficiency: unaware of our inadequacy

affection: deep love

encounters: meetings

royally attorneyed: performed by representatives of the kings

vast: a wide expanse of land or sea

matter: valid reason
of your young prince: Modern English would say 'in your young prince' (see p. 19)
physics the subject: acts like beneficial medicine on all the subjects in Sicilia

---

Act I Scene 2

Polixenes announces that he must return to Bohemia which he left nine months ago. Leontes urges him to stay longer but Polixenes insists that his visit must end. Leontes asks his wife, Hermione, to plead with Polixenes to stay. Hermione tells Polixenes that he must stay either as her guest or as her prisoner. Eventually Polixenes is persuaded to stay a little longer. Leontes is surprised that Hermione has succeeded where he failed and he is struck by the suspicion that Polixenes and Hermione are lovers.

Leontes's jealousy is totally unfounded but it blinds him to reason. He tells one of his courtiers, Camillo, about his suspicions and refuses to accept Camillo's opinion that Polixenes and Hermione are innocent. Leontes orders Camillo to poison Polixenes.

Camillo appears to agree with Leontes but when he meets Polixenes Camillo tells the King of Bohemia that his life is in danger. Together they plan to leave the court immediately and in secret.

NOTES AND GLOSSARY:

watery star: the moon, which governs the tides. The fact that Polixenes's visit has lasted nine months makes it possible that he is the father of Hermione's child
cipher: zero, the figure '0'. Alone it means nothing but a number of noughts following '1' can turn '1' into '1000'
part: go away, leave
questioned: worried, anxious
sneaping: biting, piercing
We are . . . to't: Leontes is stressing that he will never tire of Polixenes's company
Very sooth: in truth
part the time: split a week, that is, 'you'll stay half a week'
I'll no gainsaying: I will not let you refuse
a charge: a source of trouble
charge: encourage, exhort
this satisfaction . . . proclaimed: this good news arrived yesterday
ward: defence
let him there: let him stay there

I'll adventure . . . week: I'll risk borrowing another week, in other words, I'll encourage you to stay another week by assuring you that all is well in Bohemia

gest: time allotted for a visit

good deed: in faith, indeed

a jar o' th' clock: one tick of the clock

I love . . . her lord: I love you as much as any wife could possibly love her husband

limber: weak, limp

t'unsphere the stars: to move the stars from their usual courses. Many people in Shakespeare's day were convinced of the value of astrology (see pp.6–7)

fees: in Shakespeare's time, prisoners who could afford it had to pay for their food while they were in prison and they also had to pay a special fee on being released from prison

should import offending: would imply that I had offended you

lordings: little lords, young lords

verier wag: the naughtier and wittier one

twinned lambs: identical in every way

changed: exchanged

stronger blood: fiercer passions

we should . . . hereditary ours: we would have been able to face the judgement of God with no sin on our souls except Original Sin

tripped: fallen into sin, erred

Grace to boot!: what next! What else will you say!

If you first . . . but with us: Leontes probably overheard this statement and he may have misunderstood it thinking that Hermione meant that she had sinned with Polixenes. Such an explanation would make Leontes's jealousy more understandable

cram's: stuff us. 's is used for 'us' in lines 91 and 94

dying tongueless: being allowed to disappear without praise

slaughters a thousand, waiting upon that: prevents a thousand other good deeds being performed

You may ride's . . . heat an acre: Hermione is still in a happy, light-hearted mood explaining that women can be persuaded by praise to do far more than they would if forced

But to th' goal: But, to get back to the point

I long!: I long to hear what you have to say

clap thyself my love: agree to be my love and showing this agreement by holding my hand

entertainment:	reception, good treatment
free:	liberal, open
derive a liberty:	take its freedom from
fertile bosom:	generous nature
paddling palms:	holding hands as lovers do
mort:	death. Leontes thinks that Polonius and Hermione sigh because of their love for each other. He compares the sound of their sighing to the sound of the hunter's horn which tells that the deer is about to be killed
brows:	this is a reference to the contemporary description of a cuckold (a man whose wife has committed adultery) as a man who has horns on his forehead
I'fecks:	in faith
bawcock:	fine fellow. The term derives from French 'beau coq' and could be used as an endearment
smutched:	smudged
neat:	Leontes is punning on the double meaning of 'neat'. As a noun, it could mean 'cattle' and as an adjective 'tidy, well arranged'
virginalling:	playing with her fingers as if she were playing an instrument like a piano
want:	lack
pash:	shaggy head
shoots:	horns
to be full like me:	to be exactly like me
o'erdyed blacks:	there are two possible interpretations of this phrase, namely (*i*) coloured clothes which have been dyed black and (*ii*) clothes which have been spoiled in the process of being dyed black
bourne:	boundary
welkin:	sky, sky-blue
collop:	flesh and blood
affection:	passion, strong love, lust
Most dear'st, . . . hard'ning of my brows:	This is a very difficult passage. Even Polixenes and Hermione find it hard to understand:

> POLIXENES: What means Sicilia?
> HERMIONE: He something seems unsettled.
> (I.2.147–8)

The best explanation is that Leontes is raving. He thinks that Hermione has been unfaithful, and wonders whether Mamillius is, in fact, his son. In this passage he is suggesting that lust can ruin happiness; it can cause people to sin in their imagination and in fact. He thinks that he has suffered because of Hermione's lust in that he is losing his senses and growing horns

fellow'st nothing: befriend unrealities, take unreal things as true

credent: believable, likely

moved: angry, upset

pastime: object of mockery

methoughts: it seemed to me

squash: The literal meaning is an 'unripe pea pod' but here it refers to a 'child'

Will you take eggs for money?: Will you allow yourself to be cheated by taking something of little value for something valuable?

happy man be's dole: a proverbial expression meaning 'May he be a happy man'

He's all my exercise, my mirth, my matter: I spend a great deal of time with him; he is the source of all my laughter and interest

as December: as a day in December

So stands . . . with me: this boy means as much as that to me

apparent to my heart: closest to my heart

angling: trying to catch you out. By giving Hermione and Polixenes the opportunity to be together, Leontes is hoping that they will betray themselves

neb: a bird's beak, a mouth

allowing: approving

Gone already: this phrase has several possible meanings:
(1) Hermione has gone off with Polixenes
(2) Hermione has lost her virtue
(3) Leontes has lost his wife's love

forked: deceitful

play: Leontes puns on the three meanings of 'play':
(1) enjoy yourself (2) have a sexual adventure (3) act a part

whose issue: the outcome of which

hiss: criticize severely. When an actor played his part badly he was hissed at by the audience

cuckolds: men whose wives have committed adultery

she has been . . . neighbour: she has been the lover of a hypocritical friend. Shakespeare's plays often comment on 'smiling' villains, men who *seem* friendly but are not

still came home: refused to remain anchored, would not hold

It is a bawdy . . . 'tis predominant: Unfaithfulness is due to the influence of Venus (the planet associated with a wanton goddess) and Venus causes unfaithfulness in women when she is in the ascendant, that is, when she has most influence over the lives of the people on earth. It was widely believed in Shakespeare's day that the stars and planets had a marked effect on the lives of people

made his business more material: insisted that his business at home was too pressing to allow him to stay on

they're here with me already: already people know my position, people are aware that I am a cuckold

rounding: whispering (possibly with malice)

Sicilia is a so-forth: Leontes, King of Sicilia, is a cuckold

gust it: realise it, become aware of it

but so it is: but as it so happens

Was this taken . . . purblind: Was the situation understood by anyone other than yourself? Perhaps it was only understood by the more intelligent people and perhaps the common people are still unaware of it. Notice that Leontes uses 'thou' to Camillo but is adressed as 'you'

blocks: blockheads

lower messes: people of lower rank

purblind: totally blind

chamber-counsels: private and personal affairs

cleansed my bosom: acted like a priest and heard my most private thoughts and actions

we: I (Leontes is using the royal plural)

to bide upon 't: to elaborate; to continue with my charge that you are lacking in honesty

hoxes: hamstrings, attacks and undermines

grafted in my serious trust: trusted with my most intimate secrets

free: without guilt

sometime puts forth: will be made public at some time

industriously: deliberately, intentionally

not weighing well the end: not giving careful consideration to the outcome

allowed: excusable

eyeglass: pupil of the eye

slippery: unfaithful

hobby-horse: a loose woman, a whore

flax-wench: country girl employed to harvest flax

clouded so: defiled in such a way, blackened

that puts to . . . troth-plight: who allows her fiancé to make love to her before the marriage has taken place

present: immediate

which to reiterate . . . though true: to repeat which would be a sin as terrible as the one you accuse the queen of, even if that accusation happened to be true

note: sign

honesty: chastity

pin and web: cataract; the 'pin' was the tiny speck that appeared in the eye and the 'web' was the film that covered the eye

say it be: supposing

hovering temporizer: wavering timeserver, a hypocrite

liver: the seat of the emotions, more or less the equivalent of modern 'heart'

like her medal: as if she were a necklace

thrifts: gains

benched: raised to a high position

to worship: to a position of honour and authority

to give mine enemy a lasting wink: to make my enemy sleep eternally, in other words, to kill him

maliciously: violently

crack: flaw

dread: honoured, revered

so sovereignly being honourable: so completely honourable is she

thee: it is most unusual for a subject to address a king as 'thee'. Perhaps Camillo, who is an older man, is stressing both his intimacy with Leontes and his right to correct Leontes when he makes a wrong judgement

Make that thy question, and go rot!: if you are going to doubt my judgement then go to hell. 'Go rot' was a fairly strong curse

muddy: dim-witted

To appoint myself in this vexation: to put myself unnecessarily into this terrible situation

without ripe moving to't: without good evidence to convince me

blench: swerve, turn aside from the right path

fetch off: this has two possible interpretations (1) kill, (2) rescue. In view of Camillo's subsequent action in warning Polixenes, he may have meant (2) though Leontes thought he meant (1).

for sealing the injury of tongues: preventing harmful gossip

ground: justification

If from me . . . not your servant: Again, this statement is capable of two interpretations. Camillo says: 'If he receives an unpoisoned drink from me, then you will know that I am no longer your servant'. Leontes assumes that Camillo *will* poison Polixenes but Camillo may be expressing doubt

one, who in rebellion with himself: one who is not at peace with himself, one who is suffering from inner conflict

To do this deed: if I do this deed, if I perform this action

If I could . . . villainy itself forswear't: If I could find thousands of examples of people who had killed an appointed king and flourished, I still would not want to do it: but since there is no record of such a villain thriving, even an evil man would be well advised to avoid such an action

a break-neck: a hanging matter

Happy star reign now!: May I be directed by the heavenly powers!

warp: diminish

none rare: nothing strange or unusual

As: as if

Wafting his eyes . . . falling a lip of much contempt: turning his eyes the other way and letting his lips turn down as a mark of contempt

breeding: going on, happening

intelligent: intelligible

'tis thereabouts: something is wrong

complexions: looks

I must be . . . alteration: I must be the cause of the changes that I see

distemper: poor health and bad temper

basilisk: a fabulous creature who could kill people simply by staring at them

sped the better by my regard: got on better because of my looks

Clerk-like experienced: with the knowledge and culture of a scholar

gentle: of noble birth

In ignorant concealment: hiding something by pretending to be ignorant of it

parts: qualities

this suit: this request

incidency: incident, occurrence

if to be: if that is possible

Cry lost, and so good night!: accept that we are doomed to die

him to murder you: the one who must murder you

vice: force

the Best: Jesus Christ who was betrayed by Judas Iscariot

savour: smell

Swear his thoughts . . . standing of his body: Even if you swore by all the power in heaven and on earth that his suspicions were unfounded, he would not believe you, but will continue to believe that you and Hermione are guilty as long as he lives

The standing of his body: as long as his body can remain upright

trunk: body

impawned: as a pledge of my honesty

whisper to the business: secretly tell about our plans

at several posterns: by different small gates around the city

discovery: disclosure

Thereon his execution sworn: and sworn that the execution will take place

thy places shall still neighbour mine: your position will be next in rank to my own

hence: from here

professed: swore affection

o'ershades me: hangs over me

Good expedition . . . ill-ta'en suspicion: May heaven help me to escape, may heaven also give comfort to the queen who is also suspected, but who is totally innocent of his ill-founded suspicions

avoid: get away from here

please your highness . . . urgent hour: may it please your highness to hurry

---

Act II Scene 1

Hermione and her ladies are being entertained by the childish wit of Mamillius when their joy is interrupted by Leontes. The King has just heard that Polixenes and Camillo have escaped and their action makes him feel even more sure of Hermione's guilt. Leontes orders Mamillius to be taken away and then, before many of the lords and ladies of the court, he accuses Hermione of committing adultery with Polixenes. At first, Hermione thinks Leontes is joking and she assures him that such jokes are in very poor taste. Later, when she realises that he is serious, she behaves with courage and dignity.

When Hermione is sent to prison some of the lords try to reason with Leontes. They insist that Hermione is good and honest. Leontes, however, refuses to be moved by their pleas. He claims that he is certain of Hermione's guilt, but, to convince his court that he is right, he has sent a delegation to consult Apollo's Oracle at Delphos. With that the lords must be content.

NOTES AND GLOSSARY:

he so troubles me: Hermione's words are not meant to be taken seriously. The first 32 lines of the scene are given over to playful banter. The tone of this section is happy in contrast to the rest of the scene where injustice and intolerance predominate

rounds: gets round, gets fatter

prince: royal child, either a prince or a princess

wanton: play, enjoy yourself

good time encounter her: may she have an easy time when she is in labour

I am for you: I am ready for you

crickets: talkative ladies-in-waiting

train: retinue, followers

just censure: fair condemnation

Alack, for lesser . . . so blest: I wish I knew less. I am really unlucky in being proved right

spider: in Shakespeare's day, many people believed that a spider could poison one's food or drink if one knew that it had been put there

hefts: retchings, vomiting

discovered: revealed

pinched: tormented, tortured

trick: plaything

sport: a game

sport: behave immorally

thee: Leontes's use of 'thee' to Hermione was intended as an insult (see pp.17–18)

you learn to th'nay-ward: you are inclined to the opposite view

without-door forms: external appearances

I am out: I am wrong

replenished: absolute, complete, thorough

a creature of thy place: a person in your position

barbarism: the ignorant people

a like language: a similar form of speech

mannerly distinguishment: distinctions made according to the rules of good manners

federary: accomplice, helper

principal: accomplice (Polixenes)

bed-swerver: one who has defiled her marriage bed, an adulteress

vulgars: commoners

Privy to none of this: I was not aware of any of this

right me throughly: make thorough amends

the centre: the world (because it was thought to be the centre of the universe)

afar off guilty: guilty from a distance; that is, an accessory to Hermione's guilt

ill planet: Hermione attributes her misfortune to an astrological cause (see pp.6–7)

want: lack

charities: loves, sense of kindness

heard: heard and obeyed

good fools: good, innocent women. The expression 'good fool' was a term of endearment, not reproach

action: legal accusation

If it prove . . . trust her: If it turns out that Hermione has been unfaithful I'll lock up my wife as I do my mares; I'll never let her out of my sight and will only trust her when I can see and touch her

abused: deceived, led astray

putter-on: a person who has made up the story of Hermione's adultery, a liar

land-damn him: make him suffer for his offence. It is not certain what precise meaning 'land-damn' had in Shakespeare's day. It may have meant 'thrash' or 'publish his offence throughout the land', but it is clear from the context that Antigonus meant he would punish the offender severely for his lies about the Queen

some five: about five years old

To bring false generations: to bring bastards into the world

glib: geld, make myself a eunuch

As you feel doing thus: as you may feel this action of mine. It is possible that Leontes hits Antigonus at this point. Antigonus would thus 'feel' the blow as Leontes feels the shame of Hermione's action

The instruments that feel: the fingers that have inflicted the blow

dungy earth: base, unbeautiful world

lack I credit?: am I not believed?

ground: matter

our forceful instigation: my strong belief

calls not: does not need

if you, or stupefied . . . in skill: if you are either so stupid or are using your skill to appear stupid

Relish a truth: appreciate the truth

Properly ours: by right my own

more overture: further publicity, any more exposure

by age: because of your age

familiarity: obvious intimacy

as ever touched conjecture: as any that ever aroused suspicion
nought for approbation: nothing as far as proof is concerned
all other ... to th' deed: all the circumstantial evidence confirmed that
the sin (the adultery) was committed
wild: rash, hasty
Delphos: Delphi was a town in central Greece which had an
Oracle dedicated to Apollo, the god of music and
poetry. The Oracle was renowned throughout the
ancient classical world. Apollo was believed to have
been born on the island of Delos, sometimes refer-
red to as 'Delphos' in Shakespeare's day. It too had
an Oracle. It would appear from another reference
in the play:

The climate's delicate, the air most sweet,
Fertile the *isle*, the temple much surpassing
The common praise it bears
(III.1.1–3)

that Shakespeare was thinking of the island Oracle,
though he may have combined the place names of
'Delphi' and 'Delos'. His intention was to stress the
importance of the Oracle rather than to emphasise
its geographical location
of stuffed sufficiency: to be extremely capable
all: the full truth
had: once received
From our free person she should be confined: she should be put in prison,
away from me though normally I am accessible
(free) to everyone
Lest that the treachery ... to perform: There are two possible interpretations here: (1) so that she is unable to escape as
Polixenes and Camillo have, and (2) so that she
cannot carry out the plot to kill me which was
hatched by Camillo and Polixenes. Leontes may be
suggesting that Polixenes had planned to murder
him
raise us all: rouse us all, cause us all much consternation

Act II Scene 2

Paulina, the wife of Antigonus, tries to visit Hermione in prison but the
gaoler has strict instructions not to let her in. The gaoler offers to bring
Emilia, one of Hermione's ladies-in-waiting, to talk to Paulina but
insists that they must talk in his presence.

Emilia tells Paulina that the Queen's afflictions caused her to go into labour prematurely and that she has given birth to a daughter. Paulina offers to take the baby to Leontes in the hope that its innocence will move him to pity.

NOTES AND GLOSSARY:

Let him have knowledge: let him be told

To the contrary I have express commandment: I have express commandment to the contrary, that is, I have strict orders not to let anyone visit the Queen

ado: a strange business

honesty and honour: a woman who epitomises honesty and honour

gentle visitors: visitors of noble birth

To put apart: to send away

Here's such ado ... passes colouring: there's an attempt being made here to make something pure appear to be extremely corrupt; 'passes colouring' could mean either (1) it surpasses the darkest stain or (2) it goes beyond belief

on her frights: because of her frights

Lusty, and like to live: strong and likely to live

lunes: fits of madness thought to be brought on by the moon

beshrew: a fairly strong oath (see p.62)

blister: according to popular belief the tongue blistered when a person told a lie

trumpet: the red-coated messenger who often carried bad news

free: generous

a thriving issue: a successful conclusion

presently: immediately

hammered of: thought seriously about

tempt a minister ... be denied: risk asking a person of importance in case she would be refused

wit: wisdom, intelligence

come something nearer: come closer

to pass it: to let it pass

process: according to legal procedure

if any be: if there is any guilt

Act II Scene 3

Leontes cannot rest or sleep. He regrets that Polixenes has escaped and hopes that when Hermione is punished he will feel more content. He is also worried about his son, Mamillius, who has been ill since Leontes put Hermione in prison.

Paulina forces her way into the king's presence and tries to convince him that the child in her arms is his. Leontes is furious with Paulina, refuses to listen to reason and describes Hermione's daughter as a 'bastard'. Paulina leaves the child with Leontes, trusting that he may come to his senses. Leontes, however, commands Paulina's husband, Antigonus, to have the child burnt to death. Antigonus and the other lords plead for the child's life but Leontes is adamant that he does not want to:

> . . . live on to see this bastard kneel
> And call me father.
> (II.3.154–5)

Antigonus is ordered to take the child and leave her to perish in:

> . . . some remote and desert place
> (II.3.175).

Sadly, Antigonus leaves to obey the king's order. As he leaves a servant tells Leontes that his messengers have returned from Delphos with the Oracle's decision.

NOTES AND GLOSSARY:

harlot: lascivious, wanton, immoral. In Shakespeare's time, the word could apply to men as well as women

out of the blank . . . of the brain: beyond the reach of my vengeance. A 'blank' was the bull's eye on a shooting target and a 'level' was the aim

she I can hook to me: I can capture and punish her

moiety: portion, part

is discharged: has left him

the shame on 't: the shame of it

solely: entirely alone

parties: friends, allies

present: immediate

be second to me: help me, support me. A 'second' was usually a friend who assisted one in a contest or duel

free: innocent

humour: mood, mental state. According to ancient and medieval belief, there were four main fluids (or humours) in the body. They were blood, phlegm, choler and melancholy. A person's character and mental qualities were determined by the proportions of these humours in an individual's body

come at him: come into his presence
heavings: sighs
presses: keeps
gossips: godparents, sponsors in baptism
Commit me for committing honour: put me in prison for doing something honourable
La: an exclamation, possibly derived from 'Lord' (see p.62)
Less appear so, in comforting your evils: appear less obedient because I do not support your evil actions
would by combat make her good: would fight a duel in defence of her goodness
the worst: the poorest fighter
that makes but trifles of his eyes: who does not value his eyes. Paulina is saying that she will scratch out the eyes of the first man who touches her
mankind: masculine
A most intelligencing bawd: a prostitute who acts as a go-between. Leontes is accusing Paulina of carrying messages between Polixenes and Hermione
ignorant: uninformed, innocent
Thou dotard!: you fool! Leontes addresses this remark to Paulina's husband, Antigonus
woman-tired: henpecked (literally, torn apart by your wife)
unroosted: deprived of your rightful position of authority
Partlet: a traditional name for a personified hen. Chaucer (c.1340–1400) uses the medieval form 'Pertelote' in the *Nun's Priest's Tale*, one of the stories in *The Canterbury Tales* written during the 1380s
crone: old woman
by that forced baseness: under that undeserved title of 'bastard'
which is rotten: which is as rotten
callat: whore, prostitute
baits: vexes, annoys, torments
dam: mother
old proverb: The proverb emphasises that a child can often be very like its father, in its character as well as appearance
print: copy, reproduction
trick: characteristic trait
valley: the hollow in the upper lip
got it: fathered it
No yellow in't: no trace of jealousy in her mind
lozel: villain, scoundrel

It is an heretic ... burns in't: Paulina stresses that it is Leontes, not herself, who is guilty of untruthfulness because he,
who would be responsible for making the fire, is
sinful rather than she who would be burning in it

weak-hinged fancy: unbalanced imagination

Jove: the King of the Roman gods (see p.62)

What needs these hands?: it is not necessary to use force to make me go

by good testimony: with good proof/evidence

encounter with: risk, challenge

proper: own

thou set'st on thy wife: you told your wife to attack me

give us better credit: you should think more highly of us

foul issue: terrible result

It shall not neither: It shall not live to call me 'Father'. The double
negative was not ungrammatical in Shakespeare's
day (see p.19)

Lady Margery: another name applied to a hen. Leontes is con-
temptuously referring to Paulina

this beard's grey: Leontes can hardly be referring to his own beard
since according to himself (I.2.155) he is only
twenty-three years older than Mamillius. He may
be pulling Antigonus's beard as he speaks

adventure: risk

pawn: pledge

fail: failure

to it own: to its own. The use of 'its' as a possessive was rare
in Shakespeare's day

favour: treatment

commend it strangely: take it as a foreigner

kites and ravens: carrion birds. Antigonus may be thinking of a
passage in the Bible (Book of Kings 1:17) where
Elijah becomes an outcast and is fed by ravens

wolves and bears: numerous stories are told of children being brought
up by wild animals. The best known is the story of
Romulus and Remus who were discovered and
raised by a she-wolf

like offices of pity: similar acts of kindness

require: deserve

condemned to loss: condemned to die

posts: messengers

beyond account: hardly credible, unbelievable

suddenly: speedily

session: public court of justice

just: fair

Act III Scene 1

Cleomenes and Dion have visited the Oracle of Apollo. They have been greatly impressed by the beauty of the island and by the pomp and splendour surrounding the Oracle. Neither man approves of the accusations against Hermione but both of them firmly believe that the Oracle's message will reveal the truth. Accordingly, they hurry back to the court.

NOTES AND GLOSSARY:

the isle: in the ancient world there were two Oracles dedicated to Apollo. One was in Delphi and one on the island of Delos. It is clear from this scene that Shakespeare was referring to the island Oracle

ear-deaf'ning: the voices of the gods were often associated with thunder

The time is worth the use on't: the time has been well spent

The violent carriage of it: the rushed way Hermione's case is being dealt with

divine: priest

discover: reveal, show

And gracious be the issue: and may the result of our visit be happy

Act III Scene 2

Leontes opens the session of court which will try Hermione and states that he is only interested in establishing the truth. Hermione is accused of three crimes (1) adultery with Polixenes, (2) plotting with Camillo to murder Leontes and (3) helping Polixenes and Camillo to escape. Hermione denies the charges and speaks to Leontes with courage and with dignity, claiming that she is fighting not for her life but for her honour. She insists that Polixenes and Camillo were both good men and equally innocent of the crimes of which they have been accused. Finally, since Leontes refuses to believe her, Hermione appeals to Apollo, saying that she will abide by the judgement of his Oracle.

At this point, the messengers who have been to the Oracle are brought in. Apollo's judgement is read and it proclaims that Hermione, Polixenes and Camillo are all innocent of the crimes they have been charged with, that Leontes is a 'jealous tyrant' and the true father of the child and that Leontes will live 'without an heir' if the child is not found.

Leontes refuses to accept Apollo's judgement, insisting that:

There is no truth at all i' th' Oracle
(III.2.140)

but no sooner has he spoken than a servant brings word that his son, Mamillius, is dead. Hermione faints when she hears the news of her son's death and is taken out of court by her ladies-in-waiting and Paulina. Leontes realises his folly and appreciates that he alone is guilty of evil thoughts and evil actions. But his punishment has not ended. Paulina returns to the court to tell Leontes that Hermione is dead. She accuses him of being a cruel tyrant and Leontes accepts the justice of the accusation. His jealousy has cost him his wife, his son, his daughter, his friend Polixenes and his counsellor Camillo. He acknowledges his guilt and promises that he will visit the chapel where his wife and son are buried every day for the rest of his life.

NOTES AND GLOSSARY:

pushes 'gainst our heart: goes against my desires
purgation: acquittal
pretence: purpose, plot
but that: nothing except that
boot: help
blush: become apparent
which is more . . . can pattern: there is no other case in history which matches my unhappiness
to take: to charm, to delight, to enthrall
which own: who owns, who can claim
to prate: to talk idly, to chatter
For life, . . . would spare): As for my life, I value it as I value grief (I would be glad to give it up)
for honour . . . I stand for: but my honour is something that I pass on to my children and so I shall fight for my honour
encounter: action, activity
uncurrent: unusual and base
strained: overdone, struggled
bound: limit, boundary
gainsay: deny
not due to me: that cannot apply to me
More than mistress . . . At all acknowledge: I will not admit to being guilty of anything other than simple, human faults
as in honour he required: as, in view of his position, was only right
though it be dished . . . to try how: even if it was put before me to sample; in other words, I have never been involved in a conspiracy and would not even know how to get involved in one
wotting: knowing, if they know
dreams: delusions, imagination, nightmares
of your fact: who have committed similar crimes

concerns more than avails: will hinder more than it will help
like to itself: as a bastard deserves
easiest: most merciful
bug: terror, ghost-story
commodity: comfort, advantage
I do give lost: I count as lost
starred most unluckily: born at such an inauspicious time
it: its
haled: taken, dragged
post: post on which notices can be displayed, notice-board
strumpet: adulteress, whore
immodest: excessive, immoderate
'longs: belongs
of all fashion: of all ranks
strength of limit: strength that returns to a woman some time after childbirth
no life: I am not asking for my life
I prize it not a straw: to me it is worthless
free: exonerate, free from the suggestion of guilt
proofs: reliable evidence
rigour and not law: harshness rather than justice
flatness: extensiveness, completeness
to report it: for reporting it
with mere conceit . . . queen's speed: merely by thinking and worrying about what would happen to the Queen
New- anew, once again
tardied my swift command: delayed my order to act swiftly
though I with death . . . being done: although I threatened to punish Camillo with death if he did not carry out my instructions and promised to reward him if he did
Unclasped my practice: revealed my plot
No richer than his honour: having nothing except his honour
glisters: shines
Woe the while!: There is so much misery at the moment!
most worst: worst. Double comparatives and superlatives are common in Shakespeare
spices: samples
of a fool: just like a fool
standing by: ready to reveal themselves
shed water: cried
tincture: colour
stir: take away, remove
still: perpetual, everlasting

receive affliction:	punish yourself
fool again:	I am being foolish again
remember:	remind
upon them:	over their grave
recreation:	the word has two meanings in the context: (1) only pastime, (2) re-creation, restoration
with this exercise:	under this penance

Act III Scene 3

Antigonus has arrived on the Bohemian coast where he is going to abandon the child. He is worried by a dream he had the previous night. In it Hermione appeared and warned him that he would never see his wife again because he had taken part in punishing an innocent child. Antigonus believes the warning and he also believes that Hermione *was* guilty of adultery and has been punished by death for her sin. He leaves the child on the beach with documents relating to her background. He also leaves some gold with her in the hope that whoever finds the money will look after the child. Before Antigonus can return to his ship he is killed by a bear.

An Old Shepherd comes along and sees the child. He calls his son and they discuss what has happened. The son has seen a ship being wrecked just off the cost and a nobleman pursued and half eaten by a bear. They decide that the gold left with the child is fairy gold and that they will have luck if they keep quiet about the whole affair. The shepherd takes the child home while his son goes off to bury Antigonus.

NOTES AND GLOSSARY:

perfect:	absolutely sure
bark:	boat, ship
loud weather:	rough, stormy weather
so like a waking:	so realistic
some another:	sometimes on the other
a vessel of like sorrow:	one who carried so much sorrow
Perdita:	the Latin name means 'the lost one', 'the lost girl'
toys:	unimportant trifles
squared:	governed, directed, ruled
speed thee well!:	May you have good luck!
character:	written document telling who you are
these:	the gold coins found by the shepherd
both breed . . . still rest thine:	both pay to bring you up comfortably and still leave something over for when you are older
savage clamour:	a loud noise made by a wild animal
chase:	hunt

ancientry:	old people
boiled-brains:	hot-heads, fools
if anywhere I have them!	if I am to find them anywhere
barne:	child
child:	female child
scape:	escapade, sinful adventure
some stair-work, . . . behind-door-work:	the result of a secret love affair where the lover got to the lady either by going up the back stairs, by hiding in a trunk or behind doors
bodkin:	thin-bladed knife
takes up:	overcomes, covers
yest:	foam
hog's head:	a barrel, a large receptacle for ale
land-service:	the action that was taking place on the land
flap-dragoned:	swallowed
there your charity . . . lacked footing:	your kindness would not have been of much value
heavy:	sad
changeling:	a child left by the fairies in exchange for a human child
be rich by the fairies:	be made rich by the fairies
well to live:	rich, well-to-do
close:	secret. It was widely believed that if a person told others about a gift which was left by the fairies, then the gift would disappear
let my sheep go:	do not bother about my sheep
next:	nearest
curst:	angry, bad-tempered
on't:	because of it

Act IV Scene 1: Time's prologue

Time, personified as an old man with wings on his back, a scythe in one hand and an hourglass in the other, describes how sixteen years have passed since Perdita was abandoned in Bohemia. During this time, Leontes has endured a life of grief, not knowing that his daughter has survived and grown into a beautiful young woman.

NOTES AND GLOSSARY:

try all:	this phrase has two possible meanings: (1) test everyone and everything, (2) give pain to everyone and everything
that makes and unfolds errors:	I am the one who causes and reveals mistakes

in the name of:	acting with the authority of
sixteen:	Camillo in Act IV, Scene 2, 4 says 'fifteen'
growth untried:	happenings unexamined
one self-born hour:	one hour which I have created out of nothing
To plant and o'erwhelm custom:	to create and abolish customs
ere ancient'st order:	since before the oldest civilisations
what is now received:	the customs of the present day
seems to it:	seems stale when compared to the happenings of today
scene:	play
As:	as if
Th'effects of his fond jealousies:	the results of his foolish suspicions
imagine me:	concentrate on me; that is, forget Leontes and think about me
o'th' king's:	of Polixenes
so pace:	I hurry on
Equal with wond'ring:	deserving the amazement and admiration it arouses
I list not:	I do not want to
to her adheres:	concerns her
argument:	subject matter, theme
Of this allow:	be sure of this
worse ere now:	less agreeably than you are at the moment
yet that:	then, be sure that

Act IV Scene 2

Camillo has served Polixenes well throughout the past sixteen years and Polixenes has been generous to him. Camillo, however, feels that he would like to return home and spend the last years of his life in Sicilia. Polixenes pleads with Camillo to remain in Bohemia and says that Camillo can help discover why the young prince, Florizel, is spending so much time at the house of the shepherd. Polixenes adds that his informers have told him that the shepherd is extremely rich and has a very beautiful daughter. Polixenes appeals to Camillo to forget Sicilia and accompany him, in disguise, to the shepherd's cottage.

NOTES AND GLOSSARY:

'tis a sickness denying thee anything:	it hurts me to have to refuse any of your requests
fifteen:	In the previous scene, Time says 'sixteen'. Camillo may have made a mistake or it may have been a printer's error
been aired abroad:	been abroad a great deal

allay: comfort
o'erween: am presumptuous
want: lack, do without
without: except
considered: rewarded
the heaping friendships: the piling up of your acts of friendship
brother: brother king (Leontes)
gracious: good, virtuous, full of grace
approved: proved, clearly revealed
missingly noted: noted his absence because I have missed him
is less frequent: applies himself less often
eyes under: spies in
look upon his removedness: watch what he does when he is away
from the house: away from the house
very nothing: absolutely nothing
an unspeakable estate: very rich, a property of unbelievable value
begin from: originate from
intelligence: information
but, I fear, the angle that plucks our son thither: but I think she is the bait that attracts Florizel to the shepherd's cottage

---

Act IV Scene 3

Autolycus, a thief and a pedlar, describes himself in his song. He steals the Clown's money. (The Clown is the Old Shepherd's son.) The Clown tells Autolycus about the sheep-shearing feast which his father is holding. Autolycus determines to attend the feast so that he can steal from the other shepherds.

NOTES AND GLOSSARY:
peer: appear above the ground
doxy: a female beggar or a beggar's mistress
pale: pallor, faces made pale by wintry weather
pugging: thieving
aunts: doxies, mistresses
three-pile: thick, expensive velvet
budget: bag in which tinkers carried their tools
My traffic is sheets: I sell sheets that I steal
littered under Mercury: was born under the sign of Mercury. In classical mythology, Mercury was the god of thieves and pickpockets. Mercury had a son called Autolycus who was also renowned for his cunning and his ability to steal. Shakespeare's Autolycus thus allies himself with stealing and cunning (see pp.81–2)

when the kite . . . lesser linen: when the kite builds his nest, he may steal small pieces of linen whereas I only steal sheets

unconsidered: badly cared for, badly looked after

With die and drab: with the money I have made from dice and women

caparison: outfit, clothes

my revenue is the silly cheat: I make my living by cheating foolish people

knock: being knocked down, being beaten

for the life . . . the thought of it: and as for the future, I give it very little thought, that is, I do not worry about the future

every 'leven wether tods: every eleven sheep will give a tod of wool. A tod was the equivalent of 28 pounds/13 kilos of wool

springe: snare

cock: a bird renowned for its stupidity

sheep-shearing feast: a feast normally held towards the end of June when the sheep were shorn

lays it on: does it very well

three-man song-men: singers of songs in three-part harmony; a counter-tenor, a tenor and a bass

means: tenors, those who sing the middle parts

hornpipes: dance tunes

warden pies: pies made with pears or apples

mace: nutmeg spice

that's out of my note: dates are not on my list

race: root

raisins o' th' sun: grapes dried by the sun in the open air

I' th' name of me!: an ejaculation used to avoid referring to God (see p.62)

a million . . . a great matter: one million lashes amounts to a great deal

footman: man on foot

canst stand? can you stand?

a charitable office: a favour, a kind action (the Clown does not realise that Autolycus has stolen his purse.)

offer me no money: if the Clown had looked for his purse he would have discovered that he had been robbed

troll-my-dames: a game played with small balls on a board

abide: stay a short time

ape-bearer: a person who took a monkey to fairs

a process-server: a man who served summonses ordering people to appear in court, a bailiff

compassed: went round with

motion of the Prodigal Son: a puppet show which related the story of one of Christ's parables

living: property

in rogue:	as a thief
prig:	a tinker thief
wakes:	festivals
pace softly:	walk slowly
hot:	full
if I make not ... be unrolled:	if I don't let this theft lead to another and if I don't show that the shepherds are fools, let me be removed from the list of thieves
hent:	hold on to and climb over
sad:	serious man

Act IV Scene 4

At the sheep-shearing feast, the audience meets Perdita and Florizel. She is dressed as the 'mistress of the feast' and he is dressed as a shepherd. Florizel clearly loves Perdita and freely confesses his admiration. The Old Shepherd comes to the feast with two visitors. They are Polixenes and Camillo in disguise. Polixenes asks the Old Shepherd about the handsome, young couple and, after talking to Perdita he acknowledges that Perdita has a dignity and grace not often found in a shepherdess.

Autolycus also arrives at the feast. He sings and encourages the simple country people to buy his wares. His entertainment is followed by a masque-like episode, the 'dance of twelve Satyrs'. A masque was a stylised drama incorporating dancing, music and poetic dialogue and often making lavish use of costumes and scenery. They became popular as court entertainment in Elizabeth's reign and were frequently presented at James I's court between 1603 and 1625. Occasionally masques made no use of words but employed music and costumes to entertain the audience. The dance of the Satyrs can be regarded as a masque of this type.

Polixenes notices how much Florizel and Perdita love each other and he determines to separate them. He asks Florizel about Perdita and the young man tells him that he wants to get engaged to her. Florizel does not recognise his father at first but when Polixenes realises how seriously his son is taking the relationship with Perdita, he reveals his identity. He orders Florizel to return to court and never see Perdita again. He threatens Perdita with torture and death if she ever entertains Florizel again, and frightens the shepherd with the promise of future punishment. When Polixenes leaves, Florizel claims that his love for Perdita is greater than his desire for the throne and he vows that, in spite of his father, he will marry Perdita.

Camillo advises the prince to take Perdita to Sicilia where he will be welcomed by Leontes. The young lovers disguise themselves, Florizel exchanging clothes with Autolycus, and get ready to sail to Sicilia. Camillo admits that he is using Florizel and Perdita for his own ends. He intends to tell Polixenes where Florizel and Perdita have gone in the hope that Polixenes will follow them to Sicilia. In that way Camillo will be able to return home and spend his remaining years there.

The Old Shepherd and his son have been badly frightened by the threats made by Polixenes and they decide to tell the King how they found Perdita. On his way to the palace they meet Autolycus who is now wearing Florizel's clothes. Autolycus convinces them that he is a courtier and can, for a fee, get them an audience with the King. The Old Shepherd will not reveal his reasons for visiting Polixenes but Autolycus learns enough to realise that Florizel might reward him for keeping the old man away from the king. Accordingly, Autolycus takes the Old Shepherd and the Clown to the ship in which Florizel and Perdita are waiting to sail to Sicilia.

NOTES AND GLOSSARY:

unusual weeds:	fancy clothes
Flora:	a goddess of flowers
in April's front:	at the beginning of April
petty:	less important
extremes:	exaggerated statements
mark:	man admired by all
swain's wearing:	shepherd's clothes
pranked:	carefully dressed
mess:	position at table

Digest it with a custom: accept it as if it were customary

swoon, I think, . . . myself a glass: I think I would faint if I saw myself in a mirror

differences forges dread: the difference between our ranks frightens me

Vilely bound up:	so poorly dressed
flaunts:	beautiful garments, finery

Jupiter . . . Apollo: according to classical legend Jupiter, the King of the gods, Neptune, god of the sea and Apollo, god of the sun, of music and poetry, all transformed themselves in order to win the love of beautiful women

in a way:	in any way
Or I my life:	or I may lose my life
forced thoughts:	far-fetched ideas
gentle:	gentle lady
pantler:	person who looked after the pantry
On his shoulder:	at his shoulder ready to serve
a feasted one:	one of the guests

to's welcome:	welcome here among us
seeming and savour:	their appearance and their perfume
Grace and remembrance:	the herbs 'rue' and 'rosemary' were said to symbolise grace and remembrance
gillyvors:	carnations
bastards:	impure. 'Gillyvors' were hybrids in terms of colour and breeding
slips:	cuttings for planting
piedness:	multicoloured nature
by no mean:	in no way
scion:	a small twig taken from a tree and grafted on to another
bark:	outer covering of a tree
dibble:	a stick which makes small holes in the ground in which seeds or shoots can be planted
painted:	heavily adorned with make-up
hot:	heavily scented
savory:	a herb like mint
time of day:	age
Prosperina:	in classical mythology, Prosperine was the daughter of the goddess Ceres. She was carried off by Dis, the god of the underworld, but was allowed to return to her mother for part of each year. Her return from the underworld coincided with the return of spring
Dis's waggon:	Dis's chariot
take:	delight, charm
dim:	delicately coloured
Juno:	Queen of the gods
Cytherea:	another name for Venus, the goddess of love
pale primroses ... die unmarried:	according to tradition young virgins were turned into primroses when they died
Phoebus:	another name for Apollo, the god of the sun
oxlips:	large cowslips
crown imperial:	a tall, yellow flower
flower-de-luce:	iris, lily-like flower
these I lack:	I have not got these because it is the wrong time of year for them
quick:	alive, living
Whitsun pastorals:	festivities occurring after Easter. Plays were often part of the festivities
disposition:	character
What you do ... what is done:	whatever you do is always an improvement over the last thing you did; in other words, you are constantly improving

and for: and as for

Each your doing ... acts are queens: each action of yours, unique though it may be, appears to be a royal action because all your actions are really the acts of a queen

large: generous

true blood: good breeding

fairly: attractively

skill: cause

turtles: turtle-doves, birds which mate for life

I'll swear for 'em: I will vouch that they do (mate for life)

that makes her blood look out: that makes her blush

queen of curds and cream: queen of the dairy, queen of milk-maids

marry: an ejaculation (see p.62)

garlic to mend her kissing with!: give her some garlic to make her kisses more pleasant

we stand upon our manners: we are on our best behaviour

a worthy feeding: a valuable estate

like sooth: truthful

as: as if

another: the other

featly: gracefully

tabor: small drum

several tunes: different tunes

tell: count

millener: a dealer who sells goods from Milan

bawdry: lewdness, vulgarity

brudens: refrains, choruses

dildoes and fadings: words often used in refrains

stretch-mouthed: vulgar, loud-mouthed

break a foul gap: insert bawdy material

matter: the subject matter, song

brave: good, fine

admirable conceited: amazingly clever

unbraided: new, unsoiled

points: there is a pun on this word which had two meanings: (1) laces, (2) legal matters

by th' gross: in large quantities

inkles: linen tapes

caddisses: garters

lawns: fine linen

sleeve-hand: cuff

square: square piece of material which was inserted into a dress and covered the breast. It was often embroidered

Cypress:	black, crepe material
Bugle-bracelet:	bracelet made of glass beads
quoifs:	tight-fitting caps
stomachers:	embroidered section of a dress, reaching from above the breast to the stomach
poking-sticks:	metal rods which were heated and used to shape starched ruffs

it will also be the bondage: I shall have to buy

against:	in time for
plackets:	aprons, petticoats
kiln-hole:	part of the fireplace. It was renowned as a place which was favoured by gossips
clamor:	silence
tawdry-lace:	coloured, lace neckerchief
cozened:	fooled, cheated
parcels of charge:	things of value
a life:	on my life
carbonadoed:	scored and cut up
wives:	women
moe:	more
sad:	serious
toys:	trifles, objects of little value
neatherds:	men who look after cows
men of hair:	men dressed as Satyrs. In classical mythology, Satyrs were supernatural beings who were depicted as being half man and half goat and they often wore clothes made from skins
Saltiers:	leaping Satyrs
gallimaufry:	confusion, jumble
bowling:	a ball game favoured by the upper classes
square:	a measuring device

Leave your prating: stop chattering

handed:	handled
she:	lady friend
knacks:	knick-knacks

nothing marted with him: bought nothing from him
interpretation should abuse: should misinterpret what you've done
you were straited for a reply: you would find it hard to give her a satisfactory answer

looks:	expects
sometime:	on some occasion, previously
Ethiopian's:	African's, negro's
bolted:	sifted
force:	strength

By th' pattern . . . purity of his: I believe that his intentions are as pure as mine

yet: so far, at this stage

Contract us: arrange our engagement

reasonable affairs: matters that require reason and intelligence

alt'ring rheums: serious colds that cause his health to deteriorate

dispute: talk knowledgeably about

bed-rid: bed-ridden, confined to bed

being childish: when he was a child

reason my son: it is reasonable that my son

affects a sheep-hook: has affection for a shepherdess

of force: without doubt

cop'st with: deals with

More homely than thy state: less attractive than even your low social status

farre: further removed

Deucalion: a Greek Noah who helped to populate the world after a great deluge

churl: peasant

dead: mortal

enchantment: one whose beauty is capable of casting a spell on a young man

undone: ruined

looks on alike: looks on all without favour or disfavour

state: position

where no priest shovels in dust: in an unsanctified burial ground

adventure: risk

for plucking back: because I was pulled back

I not purpose it: I do not intend to

fancy: love

wombs: holds within it

passion: anger, fury

tug: struggle with each other

What course . . . the reporting: but where I choose to go will not benefit you to know or me to tell

easier for: more willing to accept

by and by: immediately, just now

irremoveable: incapable of being moved

purchase: gain

fraught: overcome, burdened

curious business: business that needs care and attention

as thought on: as quickly as he thinks about them

ponderous: very important

May suffer alteration: may be changed

There's no disjunction to be made: there's to be no separation

As heavens forfend!: as heavens forbid!

discontenting father: displeased father

to qualify: to placate

bring him up to liking: bring him round to accepting your choice of wife

th'unthought-on . . . wildly do: the unexpected accident of Polixenes discovering our love is the cause of our unplanned action

habited: dressed

free: generous, welcoming

'Twixt his unkindness and his kindness: between his past unkindness to your father and his present kindness to you

colour: reason, excuse

comforts: comfort and reassurance

point you forth: guide you

bosom: confidence

sap in this: good advice in what you say

undreamed: uncertain

one: one misery

Prosperity's the very bond of love: wealth and good luck make love prosper

take in: overcome

these seven years: a long time (the expression is not meant to be taken literally)

She is as forward . . . rear 'our birth': she is as far above her actual position in society as she is below me in birth

the medicine: the one who cures, doctor, physician

furnished: dressed and equipped

appear: seem so

table-book: notebook

hallowed: blessed, sanctified

in picture: to look at and steal

pettitoes: pig's trotters, feet

that all their other senses stuck in ears: that they were so absorbed by what they heard that they were not interested in what they saw or felt

geld a codpiece of a purse: cut a purse from the front of a man's trousers

whoo-bub: hubbub, noisy uproar

choughs: jackdaws, crows

discase thee: take off your clothes

the pennyworth on his side: his side of the bargain

boot: advantage, gain

dispatch: hurry up

flayed: stripped, undressed

earnest: the first part of my payment
Come home to ye: come true for you
Dismantle you: take off your mantle/cloak
seeming: appearance
eyes over: spies looking out for you
undescried: unrecognised
extempore: without planning, spontaneously
clog: encumbrance (Perdita is seen by Autolycus as a nuisance)
to go about to make: trying to make
fardel: bundle, burden
the flight of my master: Florizel's escape
excrement: something that has been separated (here, a false beard)
an it like: if it please
the condition: the nature
having: wealth, property
discover: reveal
give us soldiers the lie: cheat soldiers like us
stamped coin: good money
the measure of the court: the graceful movement associated with the court
toaze: extract
cap-a-pe: from head to foot
Advocate's . . . pheasant: Autolycus is implying that an intermediary expects to be bribed
fantastical: strange, odd
picking on's teeth: toothpicks were fashionable among the upper classes
in hand-fast: in detention, under arrest
germane: close, related
and a dram: and a little more
aqua-vitae: literally 'water of life', strong, alcoholic drink
prognostication: weather prediction
he: the sun
so capital: so worthy of capital punishment
being something gently considered: if you make it worth my while by bribing me well
tender your persons: introduce you
besides: other than
led by the nose: managed easily
case: this word has two possible meanings: (1) body, (2) situation
We must to: we must go to

gone else:	otherwise ruined
look upon the hedge:	relieve myself
occasion:	opportunity, chance
turn back:	work out
to shore them:	to put them ashore

Act V Scene 1

Even after sixteen years Leontes continues to mourn for Hermione. Some courtiers advise him to marry again and have children who can follow him on the throne but Leontes feels that no one can take Hermione's place. Paulina encourages Leontes not to marry and eventually he agrees that he will only marry a woman selected for him by Paulina.

Shortly after this dicussion, Florizel and Perdita are announced. Florizel claims that he has been sent as an envoy of his father and, although Leontes is surprised that Florizel is so poorly attended, he believes the young man's story. Everyone is amazed at Perdita's beauty when Florizel introduces her as his wife and as a Lybian princess.

Florizel has barely finished his account when a messenger arrives from Polixenes. Polixenes asks Leontes to detain Florizel and explains why the detention is necessary. The messenger adds that Perdita's father and brother are also on their way to Leontes's court. Florizel immediately realises that Camillo has betrayed him and he appeals to Leontes for help. Leontes feels some sympathy for the young lovers and agrees to speak to Polixenes on their behalf.

NOTES AND GLOSSARY:

My blemishes in them: my wrongs against them	
the all that are:	all of them
good now:	please
Have done the time more benefit: have been more useful at this particular time	
remembrance:	the continuation
fail of issue:	failure to have children
Incertain:	uncertain, insecure, unguided
is well:	is in heaven
Respecting her:	when compared with her
Alexander:	Alexander the Great (356–323 BC), King of Macedonia, who established an enormous empire and died without an heir
has squared me to thy counsel: had listened to your advice	
And begin, 'Why to me?': and ask, 'Why do you insult me in this way?' (by putting a new wife in my place)	
rift:	burst, split

Affront his eye: is seen by him
walked your first queen's ghost: if the spirit of Hermione appeared
gives out himself: claims to be
out of circumstance: lacking in ceremony
a visitation framed: a planned visit
What train?:   what is his retinue like?
Of all professors else: of all who professed another religion
proselytes   followers
Of who: of those whom
Not women: women will not follow another woman
assisted with: attended by
embracement: warm embrace
He dies to me again: I endure the agony of his death again
Unfurnish me of reason: make me go mad
print: duplicate, copy
(Though bearing misery): although my life is very unhappy
at friend: as a friend
but infirmity: except for his ill health
Which waits upon worn times: which comes with old age
His wished ability: the strength he would like to have
thy offices: your friendly greeting
behind-hand: slow, hesitant
th'adventure: the risking
climate here: stay here
graceful: good, full of grace
issueless: without children
to attach: to arrest
amazedly: in surprise and confusion
becomes My marvel: suits my surprise
in question: under interrogation
divers deaths in death: many types of torture before finally killing them
The odds for high and low's alike: the chances of success are equally
   small for rich and poor alike
in worth: in her position in society
visible an enemy: clearly an enemy
since you owed . . . I do now: the time when you were as young as I am
   now
Your honest not . . . your desires: provided that your honour need not be
   sacrificed to your wishes

Act V Scene 2

Autolycus asks a gentleman of the court what has been happening and
we learn that the Old Shepherd's documents have proved to Leontes

and Polixenes that Perdita is a princess and the heir to the throne of Sicilia. The gentlemen of the court also describe the reconciliation between the two kings.

The Old Shepherd and his son, the Clown, delight in their new-found power and wealth. The Clown agrees to forgive Autolycus for all the tricks and stealing in which he was involved. He even offers to speak to the prince on his behalf after they have seen the newly finished statue of Hermione which all members of the court have gone to examine.

NOTES AND GLOSSARY:

amazedness: astonishment
very notes of admiration: true cries of amazement
cases of their eyes: their eyelids
passion: deep emotion
but seeing: except what they saw
th'importance were: the meaning was one of
were pregnant by circumstance: supported by evidence
character: handwriting
affection: type, quality
countenance: appearance
by favour: by their features
clipping: hugging, embracing
weather-bitten: weather beaten
conduit: a water spout carved to resemble a man's head
though credit be asleep: though no one believes it
the instruments which aided: those involved in helping
of losing: of being lost
attentiveness: what she heard
newly performed: recently finished
Julio Romano: a well-known fifteenth-century Italian painter
beguile Nature of her custom: take Nature's business away by making people as life-like as Nature can
he is her ape: he can copy Nature
greediness of affection: the eagerness of love
piece: join, add to
unthrifty to our knowledge: fail to add to our knowledge
dash: trace, stain
aboard the prince: aboard the prince's ship
so: as
relished among my other discredits: done me any good because of my other failings
preposterous: in this context, the Clown meant 'prosperous'
gentle: dignified
boors and franklins: peasants and farmers

a tall fellow of thy hands: a good fellow
to my power: to the best of my ability
picture: painted statue

Act V Scene 3

Leontes and Polixenes with their children and attendants go to Paulina's house to see the statue of Hermione. They are all amazed at its life-like quality and Leontes remarks that the statue has more wrinkles than his wife had. In reality, the statue *is* Hermione. She had not died during the court scene and had been cared for by Paulina throughout the sixteen years. Hermione and Perdita rejoice in each other and Leontes is reconciled with his wife. Florizel and Perdita are betrothed and Leontes arranges a marriage between Paulina and Camillo so that they may share in the general rejoicing.

NOTES AND GLOSSARY:
We honour you with trouble: the honour you speak of is really a source
                    of trouble
In many singularities: at its many rare treasures
lonely: alone, separate
To see life . . . mocked death: to see life imitated as closely as sleep imitates death
piece: work of art
fixed: painted
So many summers dry: nor can sixteen summers dry your tears
Let him that . . . up in himself: I was partly responsible for your grief so
                    let me carry some of it for you
wrought: affected
fixture: colouring and position
presently: immediately
indeed: in truth, really
double: a second time, twice
interpose: come between her and the others
vials: containers
push: impulse
like relation: a similar story
partake to: share with
lost: dead
For him: as for him
justified: testified to
Let's from: Let us go from
is troth plight: is engaged to be married
dissevered: separated

Concluding comments

The Winter's Tale, like most plays of Shakespeare's time, has five acts. This was the conventional number of acts in a play and gave the dramatist scope to present a story comprehensively. The number of scenes in a play was less conventionalised and differed according to such factors as the number of characters in the play and the time covered by the action. In *The Winter's Tale* there are fifteen scenes and they perform several functions. They provide contrast between courtly and rustic life and between tragic possibilities and humorous activities; they help to advance the story, to create and resolve mystery and tension; they show the development of characters and allow individuals to move from Sicilia to Bohemia, from the court to the countryside. The division of the play into scenes can give the impression that time is passing. This is particularly necessary in *The Winter's Tale* as there is a gap of sixteen years between Act III, Scene 3 and Act IV, Scene 1. A personified Time explains what has happened during the intervening period and his appearance helps the transition from the hatred, dissension and evil of the first part of the play to the love, joy and reconciliation of the conclusion.

The Winter's Tale is a complex play which deals with many interrelated themes. Basic to the play is the struggle between good and evil. Jealousy can cause suffering and death, the decay of friendship and the loss of personal happiness. But balanced against the evil which resulted from the insane jealousy of Leontes is the suggestion that good can triumph over bad, conquering evil, injustice, separation and, in time, replacing them with forgiveness, mercy, reconciliation.

Towards the end of his career Shakespeare seems to have been impressed by the power and goodness of noble women. Hermione has beauty, strength, warmth and courage and Perdita represents youth and loveliness, innocence and trust. In *The Winter's Tale* Shakespeare combines his interest in the nobility of women with the theme of death and resurrection. As in his other late plays, *Pericles* and *Cymbeline*, a woman appears to die and then comes to life again. Where *The Winter's Tale* differs from the other plays, however, is in the fact that members of the audience are not prepared for Hermione's restoration. They, like Antigonus, believe that Hermione is truly dead.

Some critics of *The Winter's Tale* have suggested that failure to prepare the audience for Hermione's reappearance is a weakness in the structure of the play. Others have claimed that Hermione's resurrection is a Christian allegory underlining the belief that the body only appears to die but is eventually reunited with the spirit. There is probably some truth in both views but it is worth emphasising that in spite of the complex interweaving of themes in *The Winter's Tale* it is, above all, an effective, romantic drama that tells an exciting and moving story and introduces the audience to a wide variety of frightening, inspiring and comic characters.

To a casual reader, *The Winter's Tale* seems to fall into two sections, the first section ending with the disintegration of Leontes's family life and the second leading to the restoration of peace and harmony. On closer acquaintance, however, the play seems to have three parts. The first centres on the events at the court of Leontes and deals with the pain and sadness which human wilfulness can cause. The second part takes place in Bohemia and is largely concerned with innocence, with youthful love and with humour. The third part completes the circle in that it takes place in Sicilia and shows how the evil and sadness of the first part can, in part, be redeemed by the love and joy of the second.

In *The Winter's Tale*, as in his other plays, Shakespeare's use of ejaculations, oaths and references to God was conventionalised. On 27 May 1606, a statute was passed to prevent swearing in plays. According to the statute anyone could be fined up to £10 (a great deal of money in the seventeenth century) for profane use of the name of God, of Jesus Christ, of the Holy Ghost or of the Trinity. *The Winter's Tale* was written after this statute was passed and so we find that Christian references are minimised although there are many allusions to the gods of Classical mythology. In Act II, Scene 3, 125–6 for example, we find a reference to Jove:

> Jove send her
> A better guiding spirit!

and we also find the use of exclamations which are not immediately recognisable as swearing:

> La (Lord) (II.3.50)

and:

> marry (By Mary, the mother of Jesus) (IV.4.163).

The *Winter's Tale* is, at one level, a fairy tale containing such traditional elements as a royal baby being brought up by humble people and eventually restored to its rightful heritage, a prince who disguises himself to visit his beloved, a faithful queen dishonoured but finally restored to her husband and a happy ending. But it is much more than just a romantic fairy tale. The play examines the cycle of sin, suffering and eventual purification. It deals with a number of serious themes, jealousy and honour, crime and punishment, love and mercy, but the seriousness is not allowed to dominate the play. In spite of the discord at the start of the play, *The Winter's Tale* ends on a note of serenity. The older generations have found peace and the younger ones love.

Part 3

Commentary

Character evaluation

Shakespeare's characters are usually subtly drawn. Like living human beings they are rarely completely good or completely bad, and can show different sides of their nature depending on the people they are with or the circumstances in which they find themselves. In evaluating characters in *The Winter's Tale*, therefore, you should

(1) avoid sweeping generalisations
(2) try to support your opinions by reference to and quotation from the play
(3) consider the character's own words and actions but also give weight to what other characters in the play say about him.

You should realise that a character is capable of changing. It is therefore unfair to judge a character by first impressions. All the evidence should be considered and you should not make up your mind too hastily.

In Shakespeare's last plays, *Pericles*, *The Tempest* and *The Winter's Tale*, the dramatist seems to have been more concerned with human weaknesses and human destiny than in depicting highly idiosyncratic characters. Many of the characters, therefore, seem to represent a type rather than a unique individual. Hermione, for instance, can be seen as representative of wronged but noble womanhood, Perdita and Florizel as symbolic of youth and innocent love, Camillo as the loyal retainer and Leontes as a man whose impetuous action destroys his happiness. And yet it would be inaccurate to dismiss all of the characters in *The Winter's Tale* as shadowy and flat. They are a complex mixture of realism and idealism having many individualising features as well as having symbolic significance.

Leontes

Leontes dominates the first three acts of *The Winter's Tale* and is directly responsible for much that happens in Acts IV andV. When the audience first encounters Leontes it assumes that he is good and noble because he has inspired affection in Hermione, Polixenes and in his courtiers and subjects. Initially, he is described as a devoted friend:

Sicilia cannot show himself over-kind to Bohemia.
They were trained together in their childhoods, and
there rooted betwixt them then such an affection
which cannot choose but branch now
>   (I.1.21–4)

a loving husband:

Hermione, my dearest, thou never spok'st
To better purpose

and as a father who finds joy and comfort in his son. He endorses the
praise paid by Polixenes to Florizel by saying that Mamillius is equally
precious to him:

So stands this squire [Mamillius]
Officed with me.
>   (I.2.171–2)

The less gentle side of the King's character is soon revealed, however,
and he shows himself to be jealous, cruel, tyrannical.

The King's jealousy is sudden and seems hard to account for. It
seems likely that Leontes had never before shown that he had a jealous
nature because his unexpected jealousy suprises the members of his
court including Camillo:

Good my lord, be cured
Of this diseased opinion
>   (I.2.296–7)

and Paulina, who attributes the evil that befalls Hermione to:

These dangerous, unsafe lunes i' th' King
>   (II.2.30).

Leontes is self-deceived. Unlike Shakespeare's Othello, he has no Iago
to blame. And he is alone in his suspicions. No one else can be persuaded
to distrust Hermione. A Lord expresses the opinion of everyone at
court when he insists:

For her, my lord,
I dare my life lay down, and will do't, sir,
Please you t'accept it, that the queen is spotless
I' th' eyes of heaven
>   (II.1.129–32)

And yet, his jealousy is to some extent comprehensible. He is hurt and
surprised that Polixenes refuses his invitation to prolong his visit to
Sicilia and then accepts Hermione's:

```
LEONTES:              Is he won yet?
HERMIONE: He'll stay, my lord.
LEONTES:              At my request he would not.
        (I.2.86-7)
```

and he misinterprets Hermione's banter. When he praises her for persuading Polixenes to stay, he says that she had only once before spoken to better effect and that was when she had agreed to be his wife. Hermione jokingly replies:

> Why lo you now; I have spoke to th' purpose twice:
> The one, for ever earned a royal husband;
> Th' other, for some while a friend.
>   (I.2.106-8)

Hermione's use of the word 'friend' was unfortunate because, in Shakespeare's day, it could also mean 'lover'. Also, the fact that she juxtaposes the winning of a husband with the winning of a 'friend' kindles the King's suspicion:

> Too hot, too hot
> To mingle friendship far, is mingling bloods.
> I have tremor cordis on me: my heart dances,
> But not for joy—not joy
>   (I.2.108-11)

Soon Leontes becomes totally convinced in his own mind that Hermione has committed adultery:

> My wife's a hobby-horse, deserves a name
> As rank as any flax-wench that puts to
> Before her troth-plight
>   (I.2.276-8)

and then he longs for revenge, ordering Camillo to poison Polixenes:

> Do 't [kill Polixenes] and thou hast the one half of my heart;
> Do 't not, thou splitt'st thine own.
>   (I.2.348-9)

Leontes shows his stubborn arrogance in refusing to listen to anyone else's view. Camillo, Antigonus, Paulina and the Lords all attempt to reason with him, but their opinions are dismissed:

> Hold your peaces . . .
> Cease; no more.
> You smell this business with a sense as cold
> As is a dead man's nose:
>   (II.1.139 and 150-2)

He refuses to discuss his suspicions with anyone. For him, Hermione is guilty and if his advisors will not accept his point of view than he threatens that he will dismiss them. He reminds them that he has absolute power:

> Why, what need we
> Commune with you of this, but rather follow
> Our forceful instigation? Our prerogative
> Calls not your counsels, but our natural goodness
> Imparts this; which if you, or stupefied,
> Or seeming so, in skill, cannot or will not
> Relish a truth, like us, inform yourselves
> We need no more of your advice.
>   (II.1.163-8)

Leontes behaves tyrannically to Hermione, Paulina and his courtiers but he does not like to be called a tyrant:

> Out of the chamber with her! Were I a tyrant,
> Where were her life? she durst not call me so,
> If she did know me one.
>   (II.3.121-3)

He tries to prove that the action he has taken against Hermione is just by sending messengers to the Oracle of Apollo:

> I have dispatched in post
> To sacred Delphos, to Apollo's temple,
> Cleomenes and Dion, whom you know
> Of stuffed sufficiency: now from the Oracle
> They will bring all; whose spiritual counsel had,
> Shall stop or spur me.
>   (II.1.182-7)

Leontes, however, only intended that the Oracle should support his opinion. When it confirms Hermione's innocence, Leontes claims:

> There is no truth at all i' th' Oracle:
> The sessions shall proceed: this is mere falsehood.
>   (III.2.140-1)

and his blasphemy brings about the death of his son and the apparent death of his wife.

Leontes is shocked into repentance by the terrible results of his actions and his jealousy seems to leave him as quickly as it came:

> Prithee, bring me
> To the dead bodies of my queen and son:
> One grave shall be for both: upon them shall

The causes of their death appear, unto
Our shame perpetual. Once a day I'll visit
The chapel where they lie, and tears shed there
Shall be my recreation. So long as nature
Will bear up with this exercise, so long
I daily vow to use it.
>   (III.2.234–42)

Once he has recovered from his insane fit of jealousy, Leontes is shown to be truly contrite and virtuous. After sixteen years he is still doing penance for his sins and Cleomenes tells him:

Sir, you have done enough, and have performed
A saint-like sorrow: no fault could you make,
Which you have not redeemed; indeed, paid down
More penitence than done trespass:
>   (V.1.1–4)

His sufferings have made Leontes more considerate of others. He endures Paulina's criticism with patience and he is moved by the predicament of the lovers, assuring Florizel:

I will to your father:
Your honour not o'erthrown by your desires,
I am friend to them and you: upon which errand
I now go toward him.
>   (V.1.228–31)

His reformation is shown to be complete as he stands before Hermione's statue and humbly admits:

I am ashamed: does not the stone rebuke me
For being more stone than it?
>   (V.3.37–8)

It is also worth mentioning that he did not forget others in his moment of joy. He arranged a marriage between Paulina and Camillo so that they too could share in the happiness of the two royal families.

In *The Winter's Tale* we see how the evil of one man can spread to affect the lives of many. To modern playgoers Leontes's jealousy may seem too hasty and ill prepared for, but Shakespearean audiences were used to sudden occurrences, to love at first sight as in *Twelfth Night*, to unexpected hatred as in *As You Like It* and to a sudden desire to abdicate as in *King Lear*. Leontes brought evil into the world of the play but his jealousy is shown to be a fit of temporary insanity. After his attack, he is gentle and considerate, humble and good. He is finally reunited with the family he so recklessly discarded, but even in the reconciliation there is sadness. The blind folly of Leontes had cost the life of his son.

Hermione

Hermione does not appear often in *The Winter's Tale* and yet her spirit permeates the play. In the early scenes her sense of justice and dignity are in sharp contrast to the unjust outburst of her husband and she remains a symbol of gentle goodness to Leontes:

> . . . she was tender
> As infancy and grace
> (V.3.26–7)

until they are reunited in the closing moments of the play.

When we first meet Hermione she is lively and warm-hearted, friendly and impulsive. She loves Polixenes because he is her husband's friend and she uses her wit to persuade him to stay on in Sicilia:

> Verily,
> You shall not go: a lady's Verily's
> As potent as a lord's. Will you go yet?
> Force me to keep you as a prisoner,
> Not like a guest: so you shall pay your fees
> When you depart, and save your thanks? How say you?
> My prisoner? or my guest? By your dread 'Verily',
> One of them you shall be.
> (I.2.49–56)

She loves Leontes:

> yet, good deed, Leontes
> I love thee not a jar o' th' clock behind
> What lady she her lord
> (I.2.42–4)

and her self-confidence partly results from her belief that Leontes loves her. When Leontes accuses her of adultery, her cheerfulness leaves her:

> I have
> That honourable grief lodged here which burns
> Worse than tears drown
> (II.1.110–2)

and we never again see the vivacity that she possessed in the first act. When Leontes first makes his unfounded attack:

> She's an adultress
> (II.1.78)

Hermione thinks he must be playing an ill-conceived joke on her:

> What is this? sport? (I.2.58)

Even when she realises that he is serious she shows consideration for
Leontes:

> How this will grieve you,
> When you shall come to clearer knowledge.
> (II.1.96–7)

and she accepts the humiliation of being sent to prison with courage,
patience and loyalty:

> I must be patient till the heavens look
> With an aspect more favourable.

> The King's will be performed.
> (II.1.106–7 and 115)

Hermione's goodness is emphasised by the opinion others have of her.
Camillo defends her:

> I would not a stander-by, to hear
> My sovereign mistress clouded so
> (I.2.279–80),

Antigonus and one of the Lords are prepared to offer their lives to
defend her purity:

> I dare my life lay down, . . .
> . . . that the queen is spotless
> (II.1.130–1)

and Paulina risks the King's anger many times in an effort to get justice
for Hermione:

> I'll not call you tyrant;
> But this most cruel usage of your queen—
> Not able to produce more accusation
> Than your own weak-hinged fancy—something savours
> Of tyranny.
> (II.3.115–9)

Hermione clearly reveals her courage, dignity and integrity in the court
scene. She defends her chastity with logic and candour:

> You, my lord, best know
> . . . my past life
> Hath been as continent, as chaste, as true,
> As I am now unhappy
> (III.2.32–5)

and although she puts up a valiant struggle, she is fighting not for her
life but for the honour of her family:

> For life, I prize it
> As I weigh grief (which I would spare): for honour,
> 'Tis a derivative from me to mine,
> And only that I stand for.
> > (III.2.42–5)

When she loses her children she loses all desire to live and remains dead to the world for sixteen years.

There is little point in speculating why Hermione agreed to pretend she was dead but she reveals that she is alive when she is told:

> Our Perdita is found. (V.3.121)

Hermione does not actually speak to Leontes when they are reunited but, from the comments of Polixenes and Camillo, it is clear that she has forgiven him:

> POLIXENES: She embraces him!
> CAMILLO: She hangs about his neck!
> > (V.3.111–2)

Hermione is an example of noble womanhood, strong in love, brave in adversity and generous in reconciliation.

Polixenes

Polixenes, King of Bohemia, is first seen as a guest in Sicilia. His long-established love for Leontes is freely expressed:

> We were as twinned lambs that did frisk i' th' sun,
> And bleat the one at th' other: what we changed
> Was innocence for innocence: we knew not
> The doctrine of ill-doing, nor dreamed
> That any did.
> > (I.2.67–71)

He treats Hermione with courtesy, respect and affection, calling her 'fair queen' (I.2.62), 'O my lost sacred lady' (I.2.76), and 'a precious creature' (I.2.459). His respect for Hermione and his sense of courtesy as a guest make him agree to spend an extra week in Sicilia even though he has turned down a similar request from Leontes.

Polixenes is sensitive and notices that there has been a change in the atmosphere:

> This is strange: methinks
> My favour here begins to warp.
> > (I.2.364–5)

He is outraged when he learns that Leontes suspects him of adultery and swears his innocence, insisting that if he had defiled Hermione he would deserve the most terrible of punishments:

> O then, my best blood turn
> To an infected jelly, and my name
> Be yoked with his that did betray the Best!
> (I.2.417–8)

He knows Leontes well and realises that he will seek revenge:

> This jealousy
> Is for a precious creature: as she's rare,
> Must it be great; and, as his person's mighty,
> Must it be violent; and, as he does conceive
> He is dishonoured by a man which ever
> Professed to him; why, his revenge must
> In that be made more bitter.
> (I.2.451–7)

Polixenes is able to convince Camillo of his innocence, yet he does not attempt to challenge Leontes. Perhaps he realises that 'discretion is the better part of valour'. He certainly fears Leontes's anger, pities the Queen and shows considerable trust in Camillo by putting his safety in Camillo's hands:

> Fear o'ershades me:
> Good expedition be my friend, and comfort
> The gracious queen, part of his theme, but nothing
> Of his ill-ta'en suspicion! Come, Camillo,
> I will respect thee as a father if
> Thou bear'st my life off.
> (I.2.457–62)

Polixenes keeps his word because when we next meet Camillo, it is clear that he has the King's affection, respect and gratitude. Indeed, Polixenes has grown so dependent on Camillo that he cannot bear the thought of losing him:

> As thou lov'st me, Camillo, wipe not out the rest of thy services by leaving me now: the need I have of thee, thine own goodness hath made; better not to have had thee than thus to want thee
> (IV.2.10–13).

There is, however, some selfishness in his love because he refuses to let Camillo return home to Sicilia. It is clear that the events in Sicilia had marked Polixenes deeply. Even though he was reconciled to Leontes, he did not want to remember the tragic events of the past:

Of that fatal country, Sicilia, prithee speak no more; whose very naming punishes me with the remembrance of that penitent (as thou call'st him) and reconciled king, my brother; whose loss of his most precious queen and children are even now to be afresh lamented.
(IV.2.20–5)

Polixenes's indifference to Camillo's desire to return home is made more excusable by the fact that he is worried by his son, Florizel, who has been behaving strangely:

he is of late much retired from court, and is less frequent to his princely exercises than formerly he hath appeared.
(IV.2.32–4)

Polixenes shows no qualms about spying on his son and so he and Camillo disguise themselves in an attempt to find out if Florizel is neglecting his duties because of a beautiful shepherdess.

In Act IV, Scene 4 Polixenes is quite content that his son should have an affair with a shepherdess whom he admires in spite of himself:

This is the prettiest low-born lass that ever
Ran on the green-sward: nothing she does or seems
But smacks of something greater than herself
Too noble for this place.
(IV.4.156–9)

But he is furious when he realises that Florizel intends to marry her:

Mark your divorce, young sir,
Whom son I dare not call: thou art too base
To be acknowledged: thou a sceptre's heir,
That thus affects a sheep-hook.
(IV.4.418–21)

Polixenes's anger with the Old Shepherd and with Perdita is reminiscent of Leontes's blind fury in Acts I to III. He too threatens those who offend him with terrible punishments:

Thou, old traitor,
I am sorry that by hanging thee I can
But shorten thy life one week
(IV.4.421–3)

I'll have thy beauty scratched with briers and made
More homely than thy state
(IV.4.426–7).

It is, however, to be remembered that a Shakespearean audience would not have expected a king to countenance a marriage between a prince and a peasant. In any case, he almost immediately retracts his threats:

> Thou churl, for this time,
> Though full of our displeasure, yet we free thee
> From the dread blow of it. And you, enchantment,—
> (IV.4.433–5)

Polixenes shows single-minded determination when he pursues Florizel and Perdita to Sicilia and a certain amount of sternness in asking Leontes to detain his son:

> Bohemia greets you from himself, by me;
> Desires you to attach his son, who has—
> His dignity and duty both cast off—
> Fled from his father, from his hopes, and with
> A shepherd's daughter.
> (V.1.180–4)

His pride has been hurt by Florizel's action and when he learns Perdita's true identity, he willingly forgives his son.

There is a generosity in Polixenes's final actions. When Hermione is still thought to be dead he offers to share Leontes's guilt:

> Dear my brother,
> Let him that was the cause of this have power
> To take off so much grief from you as he
> Will piece up in himself.
> (V.3.53–6)

Polixenes has much in common with Leontes. He is capable of sudden anger and rough threats when he feels that his honour has been slighted.

Perdita

Perdita's role is essential in the plot of *The Winter's Tale* and yet she only plays a prominent role in Act IV. Her name is aptly chosen: it means 'the lost girl'. Word of her beauty has reached the ears of Camillo:

> I have heard sir, of such a man, who hath a daughter of most rare note: the report of her is extended more than can be thought to begin from such a cottage.
> (IV.2.42–5)

Polixenes, who has most reason to dislike her, is amazed by her grace and beauty:

> This is the prettiest low-born lass that ever
> Ran on the green-sward
> (IV.4.156–7)

Perdita has an innate dignity suggesting that her breeding is apparent in spite of her humble surroundings. The Old Shepherd is aware of it, noticing that she appears to be a guest at the shearing feast:

> You are retired,
> As if you were a feasted one, and not
> The hostess of the meeting
> (IV.4.62-4)

Polixenes, too, notices her latent royalty:

> nothing she does or seems
> But smacks of something greater than herself,
> Too noble for this place.
> (IV.4.157-9)

Perdita dislikes artificiality including hybrid flowers and make-up:

> I'll not put
> The dibble in earth to set one slip of them;
> No more than, were I painted, I would wish
> This youth should say 'twere well
> (IV.4.99-102)

She also disapproves of bawdy or suggestive songs, asking the Clown to warn Autolycus:

> ... that he use no scurrilous words in 's tunes
> (IV.4.215-6).

Perdita loves Florizel deeply and expresses her love openly:

> I would I had some flowers o' th' spring, that might
> Become your time of day
> (IV.4.113)

and yet she is aware that the difference in their rank is likely to bring about their separation:

> Your resolution cannot hold when 'tis
> Opposed, as it must be, by th' power of the King:
> (IV.4.36-7)

When Polixenes reveals his opposition to the match, Perdita offers to set Florizel free and worries more about the consequences to him than to herself:

> Will't please you, sir, be gone?
> I told you what would come of this: beseech you,

Of your own state take care: this dream of mine—
Being now awake, I'll queen it no inch farther,
But milk my ewes, and weep
(IV.4.447–51)

When she realises that Florizel is determined to go through with the marriage, however, she agrees to accompany him to Sicilia even though she knows the risks involved in her action:

I see the play so lies
That I must bear a part.
(IV.4.655–6)

Perdita's innocence and inner beauty are reflected in her love of flowers and in the gracefulness of the language she uses to describe them:

. . . daffodils,
That come before the swallow dares, and take
The wind of March with beauty; violets, dim,
But sweeter than the lids of Juno's eyes
Or Cytherea's breath; pale primroses,
That die unmarried, ere they can behold
Bright Phoebus in his strength
(IV.4.118–24).

She shows courage in her relationship with Florizel and a great deal of common sense. She is not unduly frightened by the threats of Polixenes though her sense of respect restrained her from saying what she felt:

I was not much afeared; for once or twice
I was about to speak, and tell him plainly
The selfsame sun that shines upon his court
Hides not his visage from our cottage
(IV.4.443–6).

She has a natural wisdom and deserves Camillo's praise:

I cannot say 'tis pity
She lacks instructions, for she seems a mistress
To most that teach.
(IV.4.582–4)

Perdita is concerned about others. Her love for Florizel does not alter her attitude to the Old Shepherd. She performs the function of hostess for his sake:

It is my father's will I should take on me
The hostess-ship o' th' day
(IV.4.71–2)

and she is grieved when she learns that he has been threatened by Polixenes:

> O my poor father! (V.1.201)

Perdita is a beautiful, virtuous young woman whose breeding is obvious in spite of poverty and lack of education. With Florizel she is symbolic of a new generation founded on love and trust.

Florizel

Like Perdita, Florizel has a relatively small part in *The Winter's Tale* and yet he represents a cure for the evils of the past and a hope for the time to come. He is cheerful by nature and wants Perdita to:

> Apprehend
> Nothing but jollity.
> (IV.4.24–5)

Florizel's love for Perdita is romantic but firm. He is aware of the difficulties involved in such a match and yet he can:

> bless the time
> When my good falcon made her flight across
> Thy father's ground.
> (IV.4.14–6)

Perdita thinks that his love will not survive the anger and disapproval of Polixenes but she is wrong. After his father's outburst Florizel shows his resolution:

> Why look you so upon me?
> I am sorry, not afeard; delayed,
> But nothing altered: what I was, I am;
> More straining on for plucking back; not following
> My leash unwillingly.
> (IV.4.462–7)

Florizel's love for Perdita is so great that he is willing to sacrifice everything for it:

> Not for Bohemia, nor the pomp that may
> Be thereat gleaned: for all the sun sees, or
> The close earth wombs, or the profound seas hides
> In unknown fathoms, will I break my oath
> To this my fair beloved.
> (IV.4.486–93)

Florizel is prepared to lie to Leontes about Perdita and himself but

when he is asked a direct question his answer is manly and straight-
forward:

LEONTES: You are married?
FLORIZEL: We are not, sir, nor are we like to be
          (V.1.204)

and in spite of all his difficulties he finds time to comfort Perdita:

Dear, look up:
Though Fortune, visible an enemy,
Should chase us, with my father, power no jot
Hath she to change our loves.
(V.1.214–7)

Florizel is a handsome, courageous prince and a constant lover.

Mamillius

From one point of view Mamillius represents the destruction of innocence by evil in that he dies as a direct result of Leontes's sin. Mamillius
is young. We are not told his exact age but descriptions of him suggest
that he is under ten. Leontes says:

Looking on the lines
Of my boy's face, methoughts I did recoil
Twenty three years, and saw myself unbreeched,
In my green velvet coat; my dagger muzzled
Lest it should bite its master, and so prove,
As ornaments oft do, too dangerous.
(I.2.153–8)

In spite of his youth, however, Mamillius is highly regarded by his
father's subjects who consider him to be 'a gentleman of the highest
promise' (I.1.35–6) and:

. . . a gallant child; one that, indeed, physics the subject, makes old
hearts fresh: they that went on crutches ere he was born desire yet
their life to see him a man
(I.1.38–40)

The young prince shows a ready sense of wit when dealing with the
banter of his mother's ladies-in-waiting in Act II:

MAMILLIUS: What colour are your eyebrows?
FIRST LADY: Blue, my lord.
MAMILLIUS: Nay, that's a mock: I have seen a lady's nose
          That has been blue, but not her eyebrows.
          (II.1.13–15)

Mamillius is thus brave, witty and well-liked, a symbol in the play of unfulfilled promise.

Paulina

Paulina is a strong, courageous woman, loyal to her friends and outspoken in her criticism of tyranny. She expresses the feelings of outrage felt by the audience in her condemnation of Leontes's blind jealousy.

Paulina is introduced after Hermione has been put in prison and the first opinion we hear of her is the jailer's. He describes her as:

> a worthy lady
> And one whom much I honour.
> (II.2.5-6)

She is resourceful and capable of swift thought and action. When the jailer is worried about letting Hermione's baby out of prison, Paulina makes a strong appeal to him:

> This child was prisoner of the womb, and is
> By law and process of great nature, thence
> Freed and enfranchised; not a party to
> The anger of the king, nor guilty of
> (If any be) the trespass of the queen.
> (II.2.59-63)

She also promises to take full responsibility for her action:

> Do not you fear: upon mine honour, I
> Will stand betwixt you and danger.
> (II.2.65-6)

Paulina hopes to achieve a peaceful reconciliation between Hermione and Leontes:

> We do not know
> How he may soften at the sight o' th' child:
> The silence often of pure innocence
> Persuades, when speaking fails
> (II.2.39-42)

but when gentle persuasion fails she attacks Leontes with almost reckless courage, telling him that he is the only traitor in the palace:

> . . . for he,
> The sacred honour of himself, his queen's,
> His hopeful son's, his babe's, betrays to slander,
> Whose sting is sharper than the sword's;
> (II.3.83-6)

When Hermione seems to be dead, her attack on Leontes is sharper:

> That thou betrayedst Polixenes, 'twas nothing;
> That did but show thee, of a fool, inconstant
> And damnable ingrateful: nor was 't much,
> Thou would'st have poisoned good Camillo's honour,
>
> . . . but the last—O lords,
> When I have said, cry 'woe!'—the queen, the queen,
> The sweetest, dearest creature's dead: and vengeance for 't
> Not dropped down yet.
> (III.2.185–8 and 199–202)

However, seeing the King's dejection, she is able to feel some sympathy for him and apologises for having said too much:

> I am sorry for 't:
> All faults I make, when I shall come to know them,
> I do repent. Alas! I have showed too much
> The rashness of a woman: he is touched
> To th' noble heart.
> (III.2.218–22)

Paulina remains the King's conscience throughout the sixteen years that Paulina is lost, ensuring that Leontes does not take another wife and then skilfully reuniting Leontes, Hermione and their daughter. Her work done, Paulina prepares to retire from courtly affairs:

> I, an old turtle,
> Will wing me to some withered bough, and there
> My mate (that's never to be found again)
> Lament, till I am lost.
> (V.3.132–5)

But the time for weeping is past and Paulina is given in marriage to Camillo so that they who endured the pain of the past may rejoice in the promise of the future.

Antigonus

Antigonus is important for what he *does* rather than what he *says* in the play because he is the one who abandons Perdita.

Antigonus is a good, honourable man who tries to persuade Leontes to think more deeply about the consequences of his actions:

> Be certain what you do, sir, lest your justice
> Prove violence, in the which three great ones suffer,
> Yourself, your queen, your son.
> (II.1.127–9)

He shows wit in his reply to Leontes's charge that he cannot control Paulina's outbursts:

> Hang all the husbands
> That cannot do that feat, you'll leave yourself
> Hardly one subject.
> (II.3.109–11)

His loyalty to Leontes makes him agree to abandon Perdita in 'some remote and desert place' (II.3.175) even though he feels horror at the action and deep sympathy for the child:

> I swear to do this; though a present death
> Had been more merciful. Come on, poor babe
> Some powerful spirit instruct the kites and ravens
> To be thy nurses!
> (II.3.183–6)

Antigonus also serves the purpose of convincing the audience that Hermione is truly dead. He dreamed that she appeared to him instructing him to abandon the child on the coast of Bohemia. Antigonus obeys the instructions of both Leontes and the apparition knowing that he will never see Sicilia again. He is only the instrument of Leontes's cruelty but he suffers death for his part in the action against Hermione and Perdita.

Camillo

Camillo's role in the structure of *The Winter's Tale* is that of arranging Polixenes's escape in the first part of the play and of engineering a meeting between Leontes, Polixenes, Florizel and Perdita in the final section.

Camillo is renowned as a good man. Even when he disappears from her husband's court Hermione insists:

> Camillo was an honest man
> (III.2.74)

He loves justice and no bribe offered by Leontes can persuade him to sacrifice his high standards:

> To do this deed,
> Promotion follows. If I could find example
> Of thousands that had struck anointed kings
> And flourished after, I'd not do't: but since
> Nor brass, nor stone, nor parchment bears not one,
> Let villainy itself forswear 't. I must
> Forsake the court:
> (I.2.356–62)

Camillo gives up his position as Leontes's chief advisor and risks his life in helping Polixenes to escape. Later, he makes himself indispensable to Polixenes:

> ... the need I have of thee, thine own goodness hath made; better not to have had thee than thus to want thee
> (IV.2.11–13)

Yet he willingly gives up his position in order to see his country again and comfort Leontes:

> ... to whose feeling sorrows I might be some allay ...
> (IV.2.7–8)

Camillo sympathises with the young lovers but shows few scruples about using them to bring about his own ends. When he realises that Florizel is determined to defy his father he admits:

> He's irremoveable,
> Resolved for flight. Now were I happy, if
> His going I could frame to serve my turn,
> Save him from danger, do him love and honour,
> Purchase the sight again of dear Sicilia
> And that unhappy king, my master, whom
> I so much thirst to see.
> (IV.4.508–14)

Florizel puts his faith in Camillo and is amazed when he learns that Camillo has betrayed his actions to Polixenes:

> Camillo has betrayed me;
> Whose honour and whose honesty till now
> Endured all weathers
> (V.1.192–4)

but the result of the meeting in Sicilia seems to justify Camillo's actions.

Camillo is thus an honest man, reliable and inventive. His role in the play is to work for justice and harmony and reconciliation.

Autolycus

Autolycus is a memorable character. He is a self-confessed thief:

> My father named me Autolycus; who, being as I am, littered under Mercury, was likewise a snapper-up of unconsidered trifles
> (IV.3.24–6)

He also possesses other, more attractive, mercurial qualities in that he is lively, intelligent, witty and musical.

The gaiety that Autolycus introduces into the play in Act IV serves as a contrast to the tragic intensity of the previous scenes in Leontes's court. His worldly self-interest seems amusing and acceptable because he is totally honest about it:

> I'll be with you at your sheep-shearing too: if I make not this cheat bring out another, and the shearers prove sheep, let me be unrolled, and my name put in the book of virtue.
> (IV.3.115–18)

Shakespeare is not holding up Autolycus for admiration but he is perhaps underlining the fact that Autolycus's crimes are small compared with those committed by Leontes and contemplated by Polixenes.

Autolycus also functions as a contrast to the romantic idealism of Florizel. The prince is prepared to sacrifice everything for his love of Perdita (see p.76) whereas Autolycus thinks that Perdita is an encumbrance on Florizel:

> The prince himself is about a piece of iniquity (stealing away from his father with his clog at his heels):
> (IV.4.678–80)

Autolycus also influences the action of the play in that he changes clothes with Florizel, thus helping the lovers to escape, and he tricks the Old Shepherd and the Clown into going on board Florizel's ship.

Autolycus is a thief but he is also cheerful, witty and intelligent. He is responsible for changing the mood of the play from sombre tragedy to light-hearted gaiety. He brings music and humour into the play and his vitality and love of life prevent the audience from judging him harshly.

Old Shepherd

Shakespeare does not give a personal name to the old man who looks after Perdita for sixteen years. He is not an idealised rustic but a man who is plagued by the thoughtlessness of young men:

> They have scared away two of my best sheep, which I fear the wolf will sooner find than the master:
> (III.3.65–7)

He worries that Perdita is a less skilful hostess than his wife was:

> Fie, daughter! when my old wife lived, upon
> This day she was both pantler, butler, cook,
> Both dame and servant; welcomed all, served all;
> Would sing her song and dance her turn;
> (IV.4.55–8)

He is totally unaware that the young man who loves Perdita is the prince
and he reprimands both Florizel and Perdita for deceiving him:

> O sir!
> You have undone a man of fourscore three,
> That thought to fill his grave in quiet; yea,
> To die upon the bed my father died,
> To lie close to his honest bones: but now
> Some hangman must put on my shroud and lay me
> Where no priest shovels in dust. O cursed wretch,
> That knew'st this was the prince, and wouldst adventure
> To mingle faith with him!
> (IV.4.453–61)

When the truth of Perdita's origins is revealed the Old Shepherd takes
a childlike pleasure in his new status, telling his son:

> Come, boy; I am past moe children, but thy sons and daughters will
> be all gentlemen born.
> (V.2.127–8)

His high position does not make him forget others, however, and he
encourages his son to speak well to the prince of Autolycus:

> Prithee, son, do; for we must be gentle, now we are gentlemen.
> (V.2.152–3)

The Old Shepherd is a kind and humble man who looks after an abandoned child. He delights in the wealth and high position that circumstances have thrust on him but he remains to the end a responsible,
dignified peasant.

The Clown

As with his father, the Clown is classified as a type rather than as an
individual. He is not a witty jester like Autolycus but represents a rural
simpleton. He is totally unaware of the humour he gives rise to, even
when he is describing such serious occurrences as a shipwreck and the
death of Antigonus:

> I would you did but see how it chafes, how it rages, how it takes up
> the shore! But that's not to the point. O, the most piteous cry of the
> poor souls! sometimes to see 'em, and not to see 'em: now the ship
> boring the moon with her main-mast, and anon swallowed with yest
> and froth, as you'd thrust a cork into a hogs-head. And then for the
> land-service, to see how the bear tore out his shoulder-bone, how he
> cried to me for help and said his name was Antigonus, a nobleman.
> But to make an end to the ship, to see how the sea flap-dragoned it:

> but first, how the poor souls roared, and the sea mocked them: and
> how the poor gentleman roared, and the bear mocked him, both
> roaring louder than the sea or weather.
>   (III.3.88–101)

The Clown is easily fooled by Autolycus. He was introduced into the
play by Shakespeare for the entertainment of the audience and can thus
be regarded as a caricature of a slow-witted peasant.

Time

Time was often personified as an old, winged man who carried a scythe
and an hourglass. Shakespeare introduced him into *The Winter's Tale*
as a convenient method of marking the passage of time and of giving
the audience the information they need to understand the rest of the
play.
    Time is distinguished from the other characters in the play by his
power to control events and by his use of language. He alone uses
rhyming couplets:

> I that please some, try all: both joy and terror
> Of good and bad, that makes and unfolds error,
> Now take upon me, in the name of Time,
> To use my wings. Impute it not a crime
> To me, or my swift passage, that I slide
> O'er sixteen years, and leave the growth untried
>   (IV.1.1–6)

Time turns the hour glass:

> I turn my glass and give my scene such growing
> As you had slept between
>   (IV.1.16–17)

By this action he marks the end of the tragic section of the play and the
beginning of a more hopeful phase.

Poetic language

The creative writer enjoys considerable freedom in his use of language in
that he can mould it to suit his literary purposes. Poetic language derives
from ordinary, everyday speech but it differs from this variety in that its
purpose is not merely to communicate facts but also to delight and im-
press its audience by exploiting the resources of the language to the full.
Poetry differs from literary prose in that it is rhythmically regular. We
can compare, for example, the regulated rhythm of:

> Sir, the year growing ancient,
> Not yet on summer's death nor on the birth
> Of trembling winter, the fairest flowers o' th' season
> Are our carnations and streaked gillyvors,
> (IV.4.79-82)

with the more speech-like prose statements of Autolycus:

> Your purse is not hot enough to purchase your spice. I'll be
> with you at your sheep-shearing too: if I make not this cheat bring
> out another, and the shearers prove sheep, let me be unrolled, and
> my name put in the book of virtue.
> (IV.3.114-18)

Imagery

It is probably true to say that here Shakespeare is more interested in the
exploration of ideas, especially those associated with sin, repentance,
forgiveness, than with the developing of a web of interconnecting
images. Nevertheless, we do find recurrent images in *The Winter's Tale*,
and, in particular, we find contrasting sets of images relating to the
cyclical nature of life, to sowing and reaping, growth and decay, health
and illness. In the first scene, the love between Leontes and Polixenes is
seen as something elemental, constantly growing and capable of with-
standing time and distance:

> They were trained together in their childhoods, and there *rooted* be-
> tween them then such an affection which cannot choose but *branch*
> now ... they have seemed to be together, though absent; shook hands,
> as over a *vast*; and embraced, as it were, from the ends of the opposed
> *winds*.
> (I.1.22-4 and 28-31)

Mamillius is described as:

> one that, indeed, *physics* the subject, makes old hearts fresh
> (I.1.38-9)

and Polixenes praises Florizel because:

> He makes a July's day short as December;
> And with his varying childness *cures* in me
> Thoughts that would thick my blood.
> (I.2.169-71)

Leontes is so upset by the thought that Hermione has been unfaithful
that he feels the whole of society is morally sick:

> *Physic* for 't there's none;
> It is a *bawdy* planet, that will strike
> Where 'tis predominant; and 'tis powerful.

> Know 't,
> It will let in and out the enemy,
> With bag and baggage: many thousand on 's
> Have the *disease*, and feel 't not.
>   (I.2.200–202 and 204–7)

and Camillo, in helping the young couple, is seen as a healer:

> Camillo,
> *Preserver* of my father, now of me,
> The *medicine* of our house
>   (IV.4.586–8)

Simile and metaphor

These are often found in literary language because they allow the writer to extend the range of his references. If Shakespeare, for example, says that love is like war or life is like a bad dream, he can then use images of war and of sleep when describing love and life. Similes and metaphors involve comparisons. With similes the comparison is overt. We say that one thing is like another or has some qualities of something else. Thus Polixenes uses a simile when he compares Leontes and himself to lambs:

> We were as twinned lambs that did frisk i' th' sun,
> And bleat the one at th' other   (I.2.67–8)

and Leontes uses another when he compares Hermione's goodness to the innocence of a child:

> . . . for she was tender
> As infancy and grace   (V.3.26–7)

With metaphor, the comparison is implied rather than stated. When, in *Macbeth*, Shakespeare wrote that the brevity of life resembled the short existence of a candle which can be put out at any moment, he was using metaphor. Metaphors are used in all varieties of language and numerous examples can be found in *The Winter's Tale*. Leontes compares himself to a sinner and Camillo to a priest when he says:

> I have trusted thee, Camillo,
> With the nearest things to my heart, as well
> My chamber-counsel, wherein, priest-like, thou
> Has cleansed my bosom: I from thee departed
> Thy penitent reformed.   (I.2.235–9)

And Perdita uses metaphor when she gives human-like qualities to flowers in:

> . . . daffodils,
> That come before the swallow dares, and take
> The winds of March with beauty; violets, dim,
> But sweeter than the lids of Juno's eyes
> Or Cytherea's breath; pale primroses,
> That die unmarried, ere they can behold
> Bright Phoebus in his strength
> (IV.4.118–24)

Word play

Playing on different meanings of the same word or on words which sound alike has been popular in English literature since the time of Chaucer. Shakespeare and his contemporaries employed word play as a literary technique and also for the amusement and intellectual pleasure it seems to have given their audiences. Many examples of word play can be found throughout *The Winter's Tale* but perhaps the clearest example occurs in Act I when Leontes uses 'play' to mean (1) amuse yourself, (2) misbehave and (3) act a part:

> Go, play, boy, play: thy mother plays, and I
> Play too; but so disgraced a part, whose issue
> Will hiss me to my grave:
> (I.2.187–9)

Dramatic irony

The term 'dramatic irony' is applied to an episode in a play where the audience can see more significance in the words of a character than the other characters can. In Act IV, Scene 4, 405–11, for example, Florizel does not know that the old guest is really his father in disguise and thus he does not understand the full force of the argument:

> By my white beard,
> You offer him [your father] if this be so, a wrong
> Something unfilial: reason my son
> Should choose himself a wife, but as good reason
> The father (all whose joy is nothing else
> But fair posterity) should hold some counsel
> In such a business.

whereas the audience realises that Polixenes is making a strong appeal that Florizel should consult him before finalising his marriage plans.

The effect of *The Winter's Tale*

The Winter's Tale raises many issues which were of interest to people of Shakespeare's day and which have continued to interest successive generations. It deals with the problems of sin, repentance, forgiveness and reconciliation. It shows the ugliness of jealousy and the misery it can inflict but the play also shows that, in time, evil can be overcome by love and constancy.

The focus of the first part of *The Winter's Tale* is on Leontes and the older generation. This shifts in Act IV to the young lovers and to Autolycus. They counteract the tragedy of the first part with their innocence and mirth. In the final act the two centres of interest meet. Harmony is restored to the older people and happiness promised to the young.

The Winter's Tale owes much of its impact to the power and beauty of its language. The recurrent images of planting and growing, harvesting and decay suggest the character of man's life and the interdependence of man and nature. Shakespeare correlates the style of language with the speaker and with the occasion. The common people, including Autolycus, tend to use prose whereas the courtly characters including Perdita almost invariably use blank verse. You should notice, however, that Polixenes and Florizel use prose when they are planning to behave in an uncourtly way as, for example, when Polixenes decides to go in disguise to the sheep-shearing feast (Act IV, Scene 2) and when Florizel exchanges clothes with Autolycus (Act IV, Scene 4, 621–44). In addition, prose tends to be used for narrative effect and so it occurs in the first scene when the audience is being given background information about the characters and again, in Act V, to describe the meeting between Leontes and Polixenes and the discovery of Perdita's identity.

Music and singing make an effective contribution to *The Winter's Tale*. Music provides the background for the shepherds' dance and for the restoration of Hermione to her family. And Autolycus's songs are so completely integrated into the text that they provide both entertainment and a social commentary for the audience.

It has sometimes been suggested that the action in *The Winter's Tale* is not true to life, that the sudden fit of jealousy, the love between Perdita and Florizel and the restoration of Hermione after sixteen years could not possibly occur in real life. It is worth remembering, however, that a marriage ends a Shakespearean comedy or tragicomedy just as surely as deaths end a tragedy. In addition, we do not look to literature for chronological precision or logical exactness. The truth which has value in a work of art is a truth which imposes a coherence on the many narrative strands that are woven together by the artist.

Part 4

Hints for study

Studying *The Winter's Tale*

In studying any of Shakespeare's plays it is useful to understand something of the times in which they were written. To have knowledge of the beliefs and concerns of Shakespeare's contemporaries and to be aware of the changes that the English language has undergone since the beginning of the seventeenth century will help the reader to appreciate and enjoy Shakespeare's works. In studying *The Winter's Tale*, it is advisable to know the text well and to be able to offer quotations in support of a point of view. But knowledge of pieces of text is less helpful than understanding the meaning of the entire play, its literary value and dramatic worth.

The Winter's Tale is a play which was meant to be watched and enjoyed, and not a philosophical essay in which every comma has significance. The title of the play gives some idea of Shakespeare's attitude to his drama. A 'winter's tale' suggests a non-realistic story dealing with strange and supernatural events. It was an account suited to the winter season in that it deals with sadness and death but also with the promise of spring.

Answering questions

There is no set of mechanical rules which a student can follow in order to produce a good answer but an answer will have much to recommend it if the following points are remembered:

(1) Read the question paper slowly and select the questions you are best able to deal with. Take your time at this stage because the results of your examination will depend on the wisdom of your choice.

(2) Calculate the amount of time you have for each question and try to keep to a time scheme. If the examination is three hours long and there are four questions to answer, then you should ensure that you spend less than forty-five minutes on each question. In most examinations all questions have equal value and it would thus be foolish to lose unnecessary marks by failing to give any of your chosen questions adequate time.

(3) Plan your answer in points before writing your essay. If, for example, you are asked to describe Perdita's character, it may be useful before answering the question fully to prepare such a list as:

relevance of her name
beautiful
innocent
innate breeding that transcends her upbringing
courageous
respectful to her father
capable of deep love for Florizel

(4) Use quotations where possible in support of your opinion. If you wish, for example, to comment on Perdita's innate royalty, it would be of value to show how both Polixenes and Camillo were impressed by it:

POLIXENES: This is the prettiest low-born lass that ever
Ran on the green-sward: nothing she does or seems
But smacks of something greater than herself,
Too noble for this place.
(IV.4.156–9)

CAMILLO: I cannot say 'tis pity
She lacks instructions, for she seems a mistress
To most that teach.
(IV.4.582–4)

The reference to acts, scenes and lines need not be quoted in examinations. They are supplied in these notes to help you to find the quotations in your own edition and to see the context in which they occur. In addition, quotations need not be long. Often a line or half a line is enough to support your claim.

(5) Answer all parts of the question but do not give unnecessary information. If, for example, you are asked to compare the characters of Polixenes and Leontes, then your answer must allow equal weight to both kings. In such a question it would be a waste of time to give a summary of the plot. A good answer gives *all* and *only* the information required.

(6) An answer should be written in the form of an essay. An introductory paragraph should examine the question. Each relevant point should then be dealt with in separate paragraphs which make use of complete sentences. And finally, a concluding paragraph should sum up your views on the given subject.

(7) If, in spite of all your good intentions, you find you have misjudged your time and left yourself only a short time to answer your last

question, it is advisable to write a good opening paragraph followed by a set of notes showing how your answer would have developed. This alternative is acceptable to most examiners but a complete set of essays is more acceptable still.

(8) Remember that your own style matters. There is no particular merit in long sentences and polysyllabic words. Keep your answers simple, concise and to the point.

(9) Write neatly and legibly. There is little point in presenting information if the examiner cannot read your handwriting.

(10) Always try to leave a few minutes free at the end of an examination in order to read over your answers and correct any mistakes.

Suggested questions and suggested answers

It is not always desirable to offer students a set of 'model' answers. In the first place, we want to train students to use their own minds and to offer their own opinions rather than to develop their memories. And secondly, a student who relies totally on 'model' answers is not likely to use his knowledge creatively. He will find it difficult to select only those pieces of information which are required by an examination question and so, much of his answer may be irrelevant. The intention, throughout this set of notes, has been to offer ideas and suggestions which the student can think about and transform, rather than to imply that there is only one possible interpretation of any event, or a single view of a character's actions. The student who uses the notes carefully will find in the various sections all the information he needs to write well-balanced answers to the many questions that can be asked about *The Winter's Tale*.

It may be useful, however, to indicate how a student should deal with examination questions and so one essay-type answer to a question is presented here as well as suggested plans for two others. In addition, on pp.96-7 a set of questions is provided which will be useful for purposes of revision.

Question 1: *The Winter's Tale* has been called a tragicomedy. Describe some of the tragic and comic elements in the play and decide which you think predominate

---

PLAN: Introduction
What is a tragicomedy?
List the main tragic elements in the play
List the main comic elements in the play
On balance, the non-tragic supersede the tragic and the play ends on a note of hope.

BODY OF ESSAY:
Paragraph dealing with the tragic elements and the potential for tragedy particularly in the first three acts: Leontes's insane jealousy, loss of Polixenes's friendship/Camillo's service, abandonment of Perdita, death of Mamillius/Antigonus/Hermione, threatened deaths of Perdita and the Old Shepherd

Paragraph dealing with the non-tragic elements: episodes involving Autolycus and the Clown, the love between Florizel and Perdita, eventual reconciliation between families and friends

Paragraph evaluating the strength of the tragic and comic elements.

CONCLUSION:
Although the darkness of the opening scenes is eventually overcome by love and hope, harmony and reconciliation, tragic echoes remain—Mamillius is dead and for sixteen years Hermione has been 'dead' to everyone except Paulina while Leontes has been leading an unfulfilled existence. For the 'loss', however, there has been 'abundant recompense' but the loss has been sustained.

ESSAY ANSWER:
The term 'tragicomedy' has been applied to plays which combine qualities of both comedies and tragedies. In Shakespearean times, comedies dealt with such joyful aspects of life as love and marriage, music, humour and relaxation. Tragedies, however, described the less attractive side of life, drawing attention to human weakness and ending with the death of a central character. *The Winter's Tale* certainly contains characteristics of both genres, or types; but as the play ends on a note of happiness with protagonists reconciled and a young couple offering hope for the future, it would appear that, on balance, the non-tragic elements predominate.

To say that the non-tragic elements predominate in *The Winter's Tale*, however, is not to argue that the tragic elements are insignificant. The seeds of potential tragedy are sown in the first act when Leontes is overcome by a jealousy which prevents him looking at events rationally. The effects of the overpowering jealousy are indicated by the language Leontes uses. Gone are the lucid statements of his first utterances:

> Stay your thanks a while,
> And pay them when you part
> (I.2.9–10)

Instead we are presented with structures which seem to be an accurate reflection of Leontes's emotional state and which are not easy to paraphrase:

Inch-thick, knee-deep; o'er head and ears a forked one.
Go, play, boy, play: thy mother plays, and I
Play too; but so disgraced a part, whose issue
Will hiss me to my grave: contempt and clamour
Will be my knell.
(I.2.186–90)

As a direct result of Leontes's unbalanced mental state we have the trial and degradation of Hermione, the abandonment of Perdita, the deaths of Mamillius and Antigonus, the break-up of a friendship and the loss of personal happiness. All of these events co-occur so closely that in the first three acts of *The Winter's Tale* there seems to be much greater potential for tragedy than for comedy.

The tragic potential of the first three acts is, however, never fully realised. The short scene involving Time acts like a brake on the tragic impulse and from this point onward the effect of the tragic elements diminishes. Autolycus appears and with his combination of wit and music, cheek and light-hearted villainy he offers dramatic relief from the tensions of Leontes's court. The lovers offer the possibility that earlier disagreements will be remedied. They face difficulties but have the strength and optimism to conquer problems:

Apprehend
Nothing but jollity.
(IV.4.24–5)

A note of possible tragedy enters the play again in Act IV, Scene 4 when Polixenes threatens the lives of Perdita and the Old Shepherd:

Thou, old traitor,
I am sorry that by hanging thee I can
But shorten thy life one week. And thou, . . .

I'll have thy beauty scratched with briers and made
More homely than thy state
(IV.4.421–3 and 426–7)

but the threat is soon lifted and is not allowed to overshadow the love between Florizel and Perdita.

Until Act V the tragic and comic elements are more or less evenly balanced but in the final scene love and goodness triumph over hatred and evil, the laws of nature are suspended as Hermione returns from the dead. The play ends with Leontes once more in harmony with his wife, reunited in friendship with Polixenes and looking forward with joy to the future marriage of Florizel and Perdita.

In conclusion, then, it seems that *The Winter's Tale* deserves the title of tragicomedy because, in it, we find both tragic and comic elements.

In view of the way the play ends, however, the non-tragic elements predominate. Few of the tragic seeds have been allowed to develop fully.
Perdita is found again and Hermione is restored to her husband.
Nevertheless, the evil unleashed by Leontes has taken its toll. Mamillius
is dead and Leontes and Hermione have been deprived of sixteen years
of joy. She has been dead to the world while he has merely lived a half
life. In *Tintern Abbey* Wordsworth writes:

> . . . for such loss, I would believe
> Abundant recompence
> (lines 87–8)

and perhaps this quotation sums up the effect of *The Winter's Tale* also.
The loss caused by the tragic elements in the play are, to a large extent,
compensated for, but there has been a loss and although the events in
the story may have made the main characters wiser, they have also
made them older and sadder.

Question 2: To what extent do you regard *The Winter's Tale* as an
appropriate title for the play?

PLAN: Introduction
Brief examination of the various possible implications of the
title
Indication given that fairy-tale elements will be present, among
them:
(*i*)   the abandonment of a new-born child
(*ii*) the concealment of Hermione for 16 years
(*iii*) the love between a handsome prince and a beautiful peasant
who turns out to be a princess
(*iv*) the happy-ever-after ending
BODY OF ESSAY:
Paragraph 1 Fuller examination of the implications of all three
words in the title
THE WINTER and TALE
Paragraph 2 The appropriateness of the title especially in con-
nection with those elements in the plot which relate
to the world of fantasy and myth-making
Paragraph 3 The inappropriateness of the title when we consider
the strong elements of realism in the play, for
instance, the evil effects of jealousy, the truth-to-
life of the pickpocket scenes
CONCLUSION:
No three-word title can completely capture the intricacies of a
work which deals with good and evil, love and hatred, sin and

forgiveness, but the title *The Winter's Tale* is an indication to the audience that some of the events in the play will relate to the supernatural and the world of make-believe. It helps the audience to accept the fantasy that is interwoven with elements that are strikingly realistic.

Question 3: Discuss the view that Leontes's jealousy occurs too suddenly to be realistic

---

PLAN: Introduction

There is certainly much to be said in support of the view that Leontes's jealousy occurs too suddenly to be realistic, but, when considered in the context of a Shakespearean play, the speed of onset is acceptable and by no means unusual.

BODY OF ESSAY:

Paragraph 1 There is no reference to Leontes's jealousy before Act I, Scene 2, 108 and there is nothing in the text to suggest that Leontes had ever before suffered from jealousy or had cause to be suspicious of his wife

Paragraph 2 There is something unrealistic in the facts that:

(*i*) Leontes's jealousy develops so quickly and so completely that he refuses to listen to the views of his wife, his advisor, his lords and courtiers

(*ii*) Leontes's jealousy is self-induced. No-one encouraged it and no-one else can be persuaded that Hermione is guilty

Paragraph 3 The speed of Leontes's jealousy becomes acceptable in view of such facts as:

(*i*) Hermione's speech (Act I, Scene 2, 107–8) is tactless (see Commentary)

(*ii*) Hermione's openly expressed affection for Polixenes

(*iii*) Speed was necessary if Leontes's actions were to be acceptable. He was suffering, as it were, from temporary insanity and under its control he behaved like a tyrant

(*iv*) Hasty decisions and speedy emotions—both love and hate—are common in Shakespeare and in folklore (see Commentary).

CONCLUSION:
> It is true that many readers and critics are surprised by the suddenness of Leontes's jealousy but it becomes acceptable in the context of the play largely because Shakespeare is attempting to show the effects of jealousy rather than its causes or its development.

Revision questions

The following questions will help with your revision of *The Winter's Tale*.

Questions dealing with general aspects of the play

(1) Critics have said that in *The Winter's Tale* little interest is shown in individualising characters, that characters tend to be flat and undifferentiated, vehicles for ideas, actions or passions rather than representations of living people. Discuss.

(2) Describe and comment on the structural weaknesses in *The Winter's Tale*.

(3) Comment on the language of *The Winter's Tale*, paying special attention to the use of imagery and to the use of prose.

(4) G. Wilson Knight has suggested that *The Winter's Tale* is among the finest of Shakespeare's plays whereas H. B. Charlton argues that in *The Winter's Tale* 'Shakespeare the dramatist is declining in dramatic power'. Show by close reference to the play why you think *The Winter's Tale* could have inspired such different responses.

(5) Discuss the significance of the title *The Winter's Tale*.

Questions dealing with specific points in the play

(1) What dramatic purposes are served by the short introductory scene?

(2) It has been suggested that the episodes involving Autolycus are extraneous to the central plot of *The Winter's Tale*. What, in your opinion, would be lost if the sections involving Autolycus were deleted?

(3) Write an account of Act V showing how the many problems raised in the earlier acts are resolved.

(4) Illustrate the ways in which Camillo shows that his greatest loyalty is to justice rather than to either Leontes or Polixenes.

(5) Describe the trial scene in *The Winter's Tale* and explain its importance in the plot.

Questions dealing with characters

(1) Select two female characters from *The Winter's Tale* and show how well Shakespeare understood women.

(2) 'Leontes improves after Act III and Polixenes disimproves'. Explain why you think the above statement fails to do justice to the complexities of the two characters.

(3) What facets of Hermione's character are revealed in the trial scene?

(4) 'Florizel and Perdita are idealised lovers, having none of the strengths or weaknesses of living human beings'. Discuss.

(5) Compare and contrast the characters of Camillo and Paulina.

Part 5

Suggestions for further reading

The student who wishes to extend his knowledge of *The Winter's Tale* and Shakespeare may wish to consult all or some of the following books.

The text

The Arden Shakespeare edition of *The Winter's Tale*, edited by J.H.P. Pafford, Methuen, London, 1976.
The New Penguin Shakespeare edition of *The Winter's Tale*, edited by Ernest Schanzer, Penguin Books Ltd., Harmondsworth, 1977

General reading

The following books should provide valuable stimulation:
BETHELL, S.L.: *The Winter's Tale: A Study*, Staples Press, London, 1947
BROWN, J.R.: *Shakespeare's Dramatic Style*, Heinemann, London, 1970
MAHOOD, M.M.: *Shakespeare's Wordplay*, Methuen, London, 1957
NUTTALL, A.D.: *William Shakespeare: The Winter's Tale*, Arnold, London, 1966
PALMER, D.J.: *Shakespeare's Later Comedies: An Anthology of Modern Criticism*, Penguin Shakespeare Library, Harmondsworth, 1971
PYLE, FITZROY: *The Winter's Tale: A Commentary on the Structure*, Routledge and Kegan Paul, London, 1969
ONIONS, C.T.: *A Shakespeare Glossary* (2nd edition), Clarendon Press, Oxford, 1953
TILLYARD, E.M.W.: *Shakespeare's Last Plays*, Chatto and Windus, London, 1958
TILLYARD, E.M.W.: *The Elizabethan World Picture*, A Peregrine Book, Harmondsworth, 1963
TRAVERSI, DEREK: *Shakespeare: The Last Phase*, Hollis and Carter, London, 1965

The author of these notes

DR LORETO TODD is a Senior Lecturer in English at the University of Leeds. She was educated in Northern Ireland and Leeds, and has taught in England and in West Africa. She has lectured in Australia, Papua New Guinea, the United States of America and the Caribbean. Her publications include ten books, among them *Pidgins and Creoles*, 1974; *Tortoise the Trickster*, 1979; *West African Pidgin Folktales*, 1979; *Variety in Contemporary English*, 1980; *Varieties of English around the World*, 1982; and *Modern Englishes*, 1984. She has written a number of articles on varieties of English, Pidgins and Creoles, folk traditions and literary stylistics. She is also the author of York Notes on *The Tempest*, *Twelfth Night*, and *Hamlet*, and the York Handbooks *English Grammar* and *An Introduction to Linguistics*.

York Notes: list of titles

CHINUA ACHEBE
Things Fall Apart

EDWARD ALBEE
Who's Afraid of Virginia Woolf?

MARGARET ATWOOD
The Handmaid's Tale

W. H. AUDEN
Selected Poems

JANE AUSTEN
Emma
Mansfield Park
Northanger Abbey
Persuasion
Pride and Prejudice
Sense and Sensibility

SAMUEL BECKETT
Waiting for Godot

ARNOLD BENNETT
The Card

JOHN BETJEMAN
Selected Poems

WILLIAM BLAKE
Songs of Innocence, Songs of Experience

ROBERT BOLT
A Man For All Seasons

CHARLOTTE BRONTË
Jane Eyre

EMILY BRONTË
Wuthering Heights

BYRON
Selected Poems

GEOFFREY CHAUCER
The Clerk's Tale
The Franklin's Tale
The Knight's Tale
The Merchant's Tale
The Miller's Tale
The Nun's Priest's Tale
The Pardoner's Tale
Prologue to the Canterbury Tales
The Wife of Bath's Tale

SAMUEL TAYLOR COLERIDGE
Selected Poems

JOSEPH CONRAD
Heart of Darkness

DANIEL DEFOE
Moll Flanders
Robinson Crusoe

SHELAGH DELANEY
A Taste of Honey

CHARLES DICKENS
Bleak House
David Copperfield
Great Expectations
Hard Times
Oliver Twist

EMILY DICKINSON
Selected Poems

JOHN DONNE
Selected Poems

DOUGLAS DUNN
Selected Poems

GERALD DURRELL
My Family and Other Animals

GEORGE ELIOT
Middlemarch
The Mill on the Floss
Silas Marner

T. S. ELIOT
Four Quartets
Murder in the Cathedral
Selected Poems
The Waste Land

WILLIAM FAULKNER
The Sound and the Fury

HENRY FIELDING
Joseph Andrews
Tom Jones

F. SCOTT FITZGERALD
The Great Gatsby
Tender is the Night

GUSTAVE FLAUBERT
Madame Bovary

E. M. FORSTER
Howards End
A Passage to India

JOHN FOWLES
The French Lieutenant's Woman

ELIZABETH GASKELL
North and South

WILLIAM GOLDING
Lord of the Flies

GRAHAM GREENE
Brighton Rock
The Heart of the Matter
The Power and the Glory

THOMAS HARDY
Far from the Madding Crowd
Jude the Obscure
The Mayor of Casterbridge
The Return of the Native
Selected Poems
Tess of the D'Urbervilles

L. P. HARTLEY
The Go-Between

NATHANIEL HAWTHORNE
The Scarlet Letter

SEAMUS HEANEY
Selected Poems

ERNEST HEMINGWAY
A Farewell to Arms
The Old Man and the Sea

SUSAN HILL
I'm the King of the Castle

HOMER
The Iliad
The Odyssey

GERARD MANLEY HOPKINS
Selected Poems

TED HUGHES
Selected Poems

ALDOUS HUXLEY
Brave New World

HENRY JAMES
The Portrait of a Lady

BEN JONSON
The Alchemist
Volpone

JAMES JOYCE
Dubliners
A Portrait of the Artist as a Young Man

JOHN KEATS
Selected Poems

PHILIP LARKIN
Selected Poems

D. H. LAWRENCE
The Rainbow
Selected Short Stories
Sons and Lovers
Women in Love

HARPER LEE
To Kill a Mockingbird

LAURIE LEE
Cider with Rosie

CHRISTOPHER MARLOWE
Doctor Faustus

ARTHUR MILLER
The Crucible
Death of a Salesman
A View from the Bridge

JOHN MILTON
Paradise Lost I & II
Paradise Lost IV & IX

SEAN O'CASEY
Juno and the Paycock

GEORGE ORWELL
Animal Farm
Nineteen Eighty-four

JOHN OSBORNE
Look Back in Anger

WILFRED OWEN
Selected Poems

HAROLD PINTER
The Caretaker

SYLVIA PLATH
Selected Works

ALEXANDER POPE
Selected Poems

J. B. PRIESTLEY
An Inspector Calls

WILLIAM SHAKESPEARE
Antony and Cleopatra
As You Like It
Coriolanus
Hamlet
Henry IV Part I
Henry IV Part II
Henry V
Julius Caesar
King Lear
Macbeth
Measure for Measure
The Merchant of Venice
A Midsummer Night's Dream
Much Ado About Nothing
Othello
Richard II
Richard III
Romeo and Juliet
Sonnets
The Taming of the Shrew
The Tempest

Troilus and Cressida
Twelfth Night
The Winter's Tale

GEORGE BERNARD SHAW
Arms and the Man
Pygmalion
Saint Joan

MARY SHELLEY
Frankenstein

PERCY BYSSHE SHELLEY
Selected Poems

RICHARD BRINSLEY SHERIDAN
The Rivals

R. C. SHERRIFF
Journey's End

JOHN STEINBECK
The Grapes of Wrath
Of Mice and Men
The Pearl

TOM STOPPARD
Rosencrantz and Guildenstern are Dead

JONATHAN SWIFT
Gulliver's Travels

JOHN MILLINGTON SYNGE
The Playboy of the Western World

W. M. THACKERAY
Vanity Fair

MARK TWAIN
Huckleberry Finn

VIRGIL
The Aeneid

DEREK WALCOTT
Selected Poems

ALICE WALKER
The Color Purple

JOHN WEBSTER
The Duchess of Malfi

OSCAR WILDE
The Importance of Being Earnest

THORNTON WILDER
Our Town

TENNESSEE WILLIAMS
The Glass Menagerie

VIRGINIA WOOLF
Mrs Dalloway
To the Lighthouse

WILLIAM WORDSWORTH
Selected Poems

W. B. YEATS
Selected Poems